SPELLING THROUGH PHONICS

SECOND EDITION

Marlene J. McCracken
and
Robert A. McCracken

PEGUIS
PUBLISHERS

WINNIPEG•MANITOBA•CANADA

Printed and bound in Canada by Friesens, Altona

96 97 98 99 00 5 4 3 2 1

Canadian Cataloguing in Publication Data

McCracken, Marlene J., 1932–

Spelling through phonics

Rev. ed.

Includes bibliographical references.
ISBN 1-895411-86-6

1. Spellers. 2. English language - Orthography and spelling - Study and teaching (Primary). I. McCracken, Robert A., 1926– II. Title.

LB1526.M33 1996   428.1   C96-920044-7

Peguis Publishers
100-318 McDermot Avenue
Winnipeg, Manitoba
Canada R3A 0A2
1-800-667-9673

Contents

Foreword

Phonics has never been abandoned by good teachers. Marlene and Bob McCracken have always advocated holistic language teaching with reading, writing, spelling, and phonics taught and practiced within thematic teaching. The issue is not whether phonics should be taught but rather when, where, how, and how much phonics should be presented. Marlene and Bob support the teaching of phonics as part of spelling. In spelling, students apply the sound symbol system to their writing. As students become writers, they gradually move from "invented" or temporary spelling to the standard spelling of words. One can plainly see the progress students are making in transferring phonics through spelling as one reads the written work of a student over a period of time.

The *Spelling Through Phonics* program has been implemented in the district in which I work. The two main strengths of the McCracken program are: (1) the immediate feedback students receive when participating, and (2) the integration of visual, auditory, and tactile modalities of learning used in the program. In other words, learning to spell is a sensory experience. Students watch and hear the teacher and are taught the placement of tongue and lips in the formation of sounds. They feel the letter sound(s) in their mouths as they continuously repeat the words they are writing for each phonetic pattern. (One precaution I would advise is that the teacher read the list of words prior to instruction to make certain that the local dialect does not alter the phonetic pronunciation of words.) With *Spelling Through Phonics* students know they are successful and want to continue spelling long beyond the allotted daily lesson time.

It is important to communicate this spelling method to parents. Many parents are accustomed to the weekly spelling list to be memorized and need to know that this practice will be discontinued. As parents become more familiar with this method of teaching spelling, they will begin to accept temporary spelling in writing as the student's ability to spell standard English is developing.

The *Spelling Through Phonics* program provides students with a developmentally appropriate framework in which to become proficient spellers and at the same time fully supports their development as readers and writers. *Spelling Through Phonics* provides the scope and sequence to support their skill development. Spelling, therefore, becomes a part of the literacy process.

Dr. R. Anna Sanford
Aurora East School District #131
Aurora, Illinois.

Preface

Children can learn to spell fairly easily if they are taught so that they come to understand *how print works*. If children are taught, they can discover that English writing is an alphabetic system in which letters are used to indicate speech sounds. With this understanding and further teaching, they can become literate. We use the word "discover" advisedly because children do not learn *how print works* by learning the alphabet and the letter sounds, and being told that English writing is an alphabetic system; they must intuit the phonemic nature of speech by being taught in ways that allow them to acquire the awareness that (1) we speak in a flow of individual words, (2) each word is composed of a limited number of sounds, and (3) the sounds of speech are represented alphabetically in a left-to-right sequence.

Although this system may seem obvious to the adult, and although many children intuitively come to understand the alphabetic nature of our writing system, too many children do not; they see spelling as a memorization of letter combinations. This makes learning to spell an overwhelming task. Further, if children fail to understand how print works, that letters are used systematically to represent speech, they do not transfer the phonics they learn to reading.

We advocate teaching reading and writing concurrently, as language skills, beginning both formally in grade one. With this simultaneous teaching, phonics is used to teach spelling as a requisite writing skill that is used naturally in reading with very little direct teaching.

Spelling Through Phonics was created by Marlene to enable at-risk children to learn about print. She found that teaching children phonics as a spelling/writing skill virtually eliminated the nonreader and the nonwriter.

First used for at-risk children, and since used extensively with whole classes, it is now recognized for teaching ESOL (English for Speakers of Other Languages) students as well. Recent affirmation of that success came in an unsolicited letter from Sherry Fletcher, who works in Maryland. She noted that ESOL pupils have particular difficulty in phonemic awareness and that *Spelling Through Phonics* helped in developing that crucial skill. She wrote:

> There is a strong sense that ESOL teachers are looking for more viable reading instruction and that phonemic awareness needs to be part of that instruction...Your work has stimulated much of my thinking and attempts to puzzle out an effective reading program for my bright, eager, but woefully underachieveing second language learners. With the *Spelling Through Phonics* program they have a surge of success, and gain confidence and real skills that sustain them through the tough task of becoming fluent readers.

This revised edition of our original work expands on the teaching rationale of the program and we hope that teachers new to *Spelling Through Phonics* will benefit from our years of experience. Most of all, we wish all the children who will learn from this teaching, "Good spelling, good writing, and good reading!"

Introduction to the Program 1

Spelling Through Phonics describes a practical, easy-to-use method of teaching children *how to spell*. Children come to understand how the letters of our alphabet are constructed to form words and how words are constructed to become text. Practice is encouraged and monitored, and teaching occurs in short sessions each and every day.

Five Beliefs About the Teaching of Spelling

The *Spelling Through Phonics* approach embraces the following beliefs about the teaching of spelling:

1. Spelling is a skill and, like all skills, is acquired through teaching and meaningful practice.
2. English spelling can be learned only to the degree that alphabetic spelling is understood.

3. Spelling is a language skill; as such it is most efficiently taught in a way that helps the learner's brain understand how print works.

4. Teaching children how to spell is the most direct way of teaching how print works.

5. Teaching children how print works results in their acquiring basic word recognition skills, which can then be transferred and applied to reading and independent writing.

Writing Is an Alphabetic System

The creators of written English did not set out to make it chaotic. Rather, they set out to spell English systematically, incorporating its more than forty sounds. Unfortunately, they chose to use the twenty-six letter Roman alphabet, limiting the representation of sound and making a completely regular phonetic system—one symbol equals one sound—impossible. Although most English spelling is rational, there are many examples of seemingly chaotic spellings of English words. These can be explained, but not to a six-year-old child trying to solve the mysteries of print. Tackling the seemingly chaotic spellings too soon can prevent a child from learning how letters and print work; until a child learns how letters go together to form words, she can never become a proficient speller of all words.

The first task is to get children to understand that English writing is an alphabetic system. When we teach children how to spell, we are having them *recreate* or *reinvent* the English writing system as the "creators" of our alphabetic system did. In this way, the children come to understand how English print works. We want to do this as efficiently as possible so that children are not confused and frustrated by the seemingly irregular spellings of English words.

Four Insights About Print

In order for children to understand the nature of the English writing system, they must grasp four basic insights about print. Children must

1. begin to understand what a word is, and then learn the convention of leaving spaces between words when writing.

2. learn the relationship between speech and print and understand that when they say a sound they write a letter. At the beginning of learning about print, this relationship must be kept simple so that children may grasp the alphabetic principle. To start the learning process we teach that when they say one sound they write one letter. We leave the teaching of spelling patterns until later, when children have a better understanding of how letters go together to form words.

3. realize that the letters are written in the sequence in which the sounds are uttered. They must learn the convention of writing in a left-to-right sequence.

4. understand *spelling patterns*. We define spelling patterns as any spellings that are not totally phonetic and when more than one letter is used to represent one phoneme. Patterns include the use of *s* or *es* to create plurals, endings such as *tion*, and long vowels with their multitude of spellings. When the concept of alphabetic writing is understood, patterns can be learned fairly easily.

Phonemic Awareness

There is great interest and concern about phonemic awareness in young children, and most evidence indicates that it is a requisite for reading, spelling, and writing.

Phonemic awareness is the awareness that:

❑ we speak in a flow of individual words
❑ the words are composed of a limited number of sounds

There must also be an awareness of how many sounds are in each word. *Cat* and *mouse* each have the same number of sounds, while *basket* has more. (William Kottmeyer recognized this in the 1940s when developing his *Dr. Spello* books for remedial reading. He considered this ability as a basic prerequisite for reading.) We suggest that children who come to school with this phonemic awareness are those who have been filled since birth with talk, and with stories, poetry, rhymes, and songs, many of which they have committed to memory.

We suspect that the alliterative quality of poetry, rhyme, and song has a great deal to do with children becoming aware of phonemes. We have commended Jack Prelutsky's *Ride a Purple Pelican* to hundreds of kindergarten teachers, who have told us that children want these poems over and over again. Charlotte Diamond, Raffi, and other entertainers who have made children's songs so popular, are helping children to attain phonemic awareness.

We strongly believe that kindergarten children should be taught language awareness skills informally: through chanting, memorizing, dramatizing, and the teacher's tracking of language. (Unfortunately, it seems to us, many school districts and parents are demanding that five-year-old children do much more. Both formal phonics and journal writing are required in many kindergartens.) Having stated our preference, we believe that children who are beginning phonics and writing must develop two basic understandings about speech and print, both of which have to do with phonemic awareness.

1. *Children need to be aware that written English is broken into words.* Written language is very different from spoken language where we speak in phrases or sentences, stopping only for emphasis. Many children, when beginning to write, show that they have not grasped this convention of written English. They join all their written words together in a stream of sounds that, to them, resembles speech. Children need lots of practice in discerning what a word is, in speech and in print. It is easy for them to confuse words, syllables, phrases, and common sayings. *How are you?* is often identified by children as one word. So we practice saying and listening until we agree that it is three words, only to then have children identify *Halloween* as three words!

2. *Children need to work with the similarities among words.* When children listen, they hear *differences.* To respond to the request, "Please pick up your hat," as opposed to "Please pick up your bat," the child pays attention to a single phoneme difference among fifteen phonemes. The child does this without difficulty, not realizing that there were fourteen like phonemes as well as the one that is different. To spell, and thus write "Please pick up your hat" (or bat) [Ples pik up yur hat], children are responding to fourteen *likenesses* as well as the one different phoneme, a very different skill than responding to differences in speech as they get meanings.

Children are not ready for written language work until they have learned oral language skills. We strongly support a kindergarten program that emphasizes oral language, thinking, and concept development and a primary program that continues the emphasis while adding the formal teaching of written language skills. Without the oral language base, learning to work with print—both as a reader and a writer—is likely to fail.

But this is not new. In 1966 Dolores Durkin[1] examined the background of children who came to school reading. She found only one common factor: someone had read to them many times. In 1975 the Bullock Report[2] noted: "...reading is secondary to and dependent upon the growth of language competence in the early years" and "Talk is a means by which they [young children] learn to work and live with one another...It is fed by nursery rhymes and singing games, by the stories that teachers and children tell and the poems they read." In 1986 Gordon Wells[3], in a seminal study, reported only one factor was of importance in predicting how well a child would read and write at age ten: how many times the child had been read to before coming to school. In 1994 Steven Pinker[4], summarizing his research about language learning, supports the notion that oral work before writing is critical, saying: "... writing is clearly an optional accessory; the real engine of verbal communication is the spoken language we acquired as children." Most recently, Dr. Ronald L. Cramer[5] of Oakland University, Michigan identifies the following six experiences that make early writing and reading possible:

1. literary exposure at home, preschool, and school
2. experience with stories, storytelling, nursery rhymes, and language play

---

1. Dolores Durkin. *Children Who Read Early: Two Longitudinal Studies.* (New York: Teachers College Press, 1966.)

2. *A Language for Life.* Report of the Committee of Inquiry appointed by the Secretary of State for Education and Science under the Chairmanship of Sir Alan Bullock, F.B.A. (London: Her Majesty's Stationery Office, 1975), xxxv, 62–63.

3. Gordon Wells. *The Meaning Makers: Children Learning Language and Using Language to Learn.* (Portsmouth, NH: Heinemann, 1986.)

4. Steven Pinker. *The Language Instinct.* (New York: William Morrow, 1994.)

5. Dr. Ronald L. Cramer. Unpublished manuscript. (Rochester Hills, MI: Oakland University, 1994.)

3. exposure to print and oral language in a nurturing, meaning-rich environment

4. being read aloud to from stories, poems, and nursery rhymes

5. a focus on children's world of meaning

6. encouragement at home and school—the intangible necessity

If being read to thousands of times is an informal way of attaining phonemic awareness—as we believe it is—then all of the above observations support phonemic awareness as a crucial factor in learning how print works.

Phonemic awareness has been around for a great many years, but it is still not taught within most classrooms or spelling programs. Reading, writing, phonics, and spelling are rarely taught in an integrated fashion. Despite numerous professional pleas to teach holistically, the recent efforts of Whole Language advocates, and the use of textbooks using a literary base, most schools still teach spelling and phonics as separate skills in separate time blocks. Schools still teach reading and writing separately. Schools rarely teach language with skills (reading, writing, phonics, and spelling) as an integral but sub-part of the lessons.

We know that teaching children *how to spell* is different from teaching them to memorize words in order to spell them. (Most adult writers know how to spell; they can spell thousands of words by merely applying what they know about print, even though the application is largely intuitive. They spell /shun/ at the end of an unknown word *tion* without even thinking about it.) Teaching spelling is best done as part of a program that focuses on content, and the oral exploration of ideas, followed by reading and writing. And with required writing, we reinforce spelling and phonics. Phonics makes sense as a writing skill; we find that once phonics is understood, children transfer and use phonics in reading as they need it.

We have found that almost all children benefit by being taught *how print works.* Even some children who come to school with lots of being-read-to experience make very wrong assumptions about print and become frustrated in trying to figure out how print works. *Spelling Through Phonics* directly teaches phonemic awareness and the understanding that the English writing system is alphabetic. Children who have been read to extensively grasp these understandings within four to eight weeks of teaching from *Spelling Through Phonics.* Other children take longer, sometimes the whole of grade one with daily teaching before they develop sufficient phonemic awareness to grasp the principle of alphabetic writing; then they suddenly blossom. However, without this understanding they never become literate.

In our other works[6], *Reading Is Only the Tiger's Tail, Reading, Writing & Language,* and *Stories, Songs & Poetry to Teach Reading & Writing,* we describe in detail a way of teaching literacy that encompasses a wide range of approaches including spelling.

In this book, we will not attempt to describe the daily writing program except to say that children in primary grades should engage in a variety of writing and recording activities every day.

Penmanship

Often, teachers ask us whether good penmanship is important, and they worry about how much they should push children to write neatly. We agree with *The Bullock Report,* cited earlier, that states:

---

6. *Reading Is Only the Tiger's Tail,* 1972, 1987; *Reading, Writing & Language,* 1979, 1995; *Stories, Songs & Poetry to Teach Reading & Writing,* 1986. All from Peguis Publishers, Winnipeg, Canada.

The ability to write easily, quickly and legibly affects the quality of a child's written output, for difficulty with handwriting can hamper his flow of thoughts and limit his fluency. If a child is left to develop his handwriting without instruction he is unlikely to develop a running hand which is simultaneously legible, fast flowing, individual, and effortless to produce. We therefore believe that the teacher should devote time to teaching penmanship and to giving children ample time to practice.

We think all children like to do things well; they like to be proud of what they do. The job of the teacher is to make it easy for children to do well. Part of our task is to make sure that the child has the correct writing tools and knows how to use them.

WRITING TOOLS

Pencils

Use normal size pencils of a good length so that they can be held comfortably. Teach children how to hold a pencil, then nag them gently to hold the pencil correctly until it becomes easy and natural. It is no kindness to allow children to hold pencils or pens in a way that will make writing difficult for the rest of their lives; that is a great disservice to children.

Paper

The size of the paper is important. (Young children need large sheets of paper for art activities, not for writing activities.) Beginning writers need only a few lines to write on; the rest of the page can be blank to allow for a drawing. We strongly recommend the use of *exercise books* such as those commonly used in Canada, Australia, New Zealand, and the United Kingdom. The book's size is just right for young hands, and the quality of the paper is good.

a.

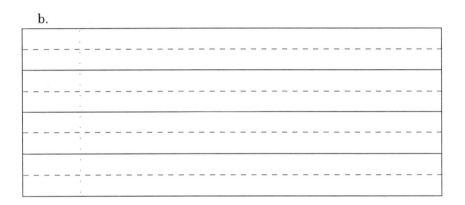

b.

Use lined paper (a) 5/16" or (b) bisected 7/16"

The lines on the paper should be of a width that allows children to print the letters, not requiring them to draw them. Frequently the paper given to beginning writers has too much space between the lines, making it difficult for them to print letters with ease. We have used 5/16" lines or bisected 7/16" lines successfully.

The quality of paper used by children should allow them to erase with ease. Erasing a mistake should not cause a hole in the paper, making a worse mess than the original mistake.

LETTER FORMATION

Children must learn how to form letters with ease so a lesson in letter formation is given with each letter we introduce in the spelling lessons. Children usually practice the lowercase form first, making the letter many times on their chalkboards. The next day, we introduce and have them practice the capital or uppercase letter. Next, we teach them how to write with a pencil and how to practice each letter several times in their handwriting books.

We believe that the formation of the letters we teach beginning writers should closely resemble the letters they see when reading. Therefore, we have chosen to use *one-stroke* letters that can be easily made by children, and that closely resemble letters found in most books. (For seven years I taught third-grade children to transfer from printing one-stroke letters to cursive writing. I had no trouble with the transfer. *M.J.M.*)

PRACTICE

Children who are learning penmanship should have a handwriting book in which they practice. The letters they practice coincide with the letters they are learning in their spelling lessons. We take two days to teach each letter, and have the children practice writing that letter during those days. The first day they practice the lowercase form, and the second day they practice the capital or uppercase form. Children write two or three lines of the letter and a row of words containing the letter that they have found in a book or posted around the room.

Children learn how to write on lines. We draw *houses* at the beginning of each line, and guide the children to write on the *main floor*, or on the *main floor combined with upstairs or basement*. We also have them draw nine or more small pictures representing words that contain the letter for the day. Most of the words will have the letter in intial position. Children like working in this little book and will work for twenty to thirty minutes daily to get the handwriting practiced and to draw the pictures. (See page 182 for a sample page of the handwriting book with houses. It may be photocopied to create handwriting books for children.)

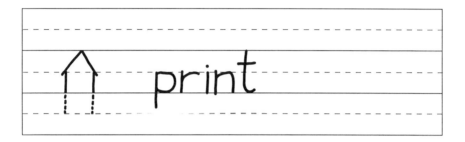

"Houses" help children write on lines

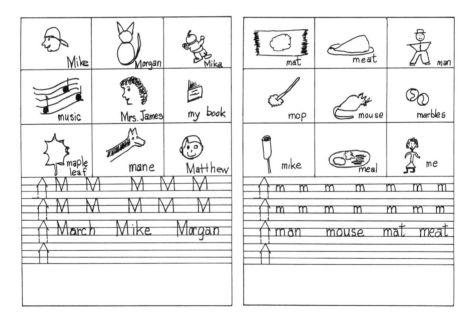

Samples from children's handwriting books

Kindergarten 2

We believe there should be no formal teaching of reading or writing in the kindergarten classroom. If children initiate reading and writing or come to school already equipped with these skills, we do not prevent them from voluntarily reading or writing; however, we do not demand that children work in any *formal* ways with print. Kindergarten should be a place where many informal activities take place that make children aware of print and of the sounds of English.

Immersing Kindergarten Children in Language

There is growing evidence that children who have a full year to explore their worlds—to be filled with language by being read to, to *play read*, to dramatize books, to sing songs, and chant poetry—move into phonics, spelling, writing, and literacy with ease and success. Withholding formal instruction, even for those children who come to kindergarten already reading and writing, does not create problems in later achievement. Our personal experience with children has been that all children benefit by having a full year of being filled with the best of language before being asked to work formally with print. We know of no solid evidence that indicates that delaying the start of formal writing or reading until the beginning of grade one, approximately age six, means that children will not progress normally and reach equally high literacy standards by the end of grade four.

Kindergarten children need to be filled orally with all of the written forms of language: songs, poetry, prose, fiction, and nonfiction. They need to memorize and sing lots of songs, chant lots of poetry, and hear and retell repeated parts of stories. They need to see and use the memorized print posted within the classroom, and they need to see print use modeled by their teacher.

HEARING LANGUAGE

Children need to hear the best examples of speech and the very best of children's literature. Books and poems should be repeated many times, allowing the words and melodies to insinuate themselves into the children. They truly enjoy hearing something over and over again. Children need time to play with the words they know so that they become an integral part of the brain's repertoire. Listening to stories, poems, and rhymes is a necessary and natural activity. It fills children with the rhythms of the language as well as the many forms of written English. Children become conversant with repetitive stories, cumulative stories, two-part stories, fables, fairy tales, tall tales, legends, and all the various forms of fact and fiction. Without this familiarity, learning to read or write those forms is rendered extremely difficult, if not impossible.

SEEING LANGUAGE

Children need to see the language they are using. We put up poetry posters, and track the words as children chant along from memory. We create poems on word cards in the pocket chart, and track as children chant. We use big books with print large enough for children to see so that they can follow along as we read to them and they join in on repeated parts. In this informal way, children learn to put what they say together with what they see. Putting speech together with print, and with literally thousands of practices, they begin to realize how print works.

USING LANGUAGE

Children need to use the language they are learning. Kindergarten is a place for children to play with language. Kindergartners read whole books or poems before they begin to recognize words. They read known material, equally well, whether the book is open or closed, because they are reading the story as they remember it. First readings by a child are rarely perfect; they are retellings of ideas and events using the child's home language. When a story has been memorized, the child's reading may sound perfect and she may appear to be reading, but the child is not reading in the way adults read. Children play with print, just as they play at winning an Olympic event, catching the bad guy, or entertaining the queen.

Drama and art are both natural ways of practicing what is being learned, ways of playing with ideas. The goal is the internalization of the language, meaning its concepts, form, and purposes. Playing with language enables children to do this.

SEEING PRINT IN USE

One of the strongest influences for kindergarten children is seeing print being created and used. Kindergarten teachers must model writing and reading, and have writing materials available for children who wish to experiment. When teachers routinely write labels, lists, names, and invite children to participate in making signs or notes as part of each day's activities, then children come to understand that print is a tool to be used and that it appears easy and natural to do so.

A Brief Checklist of Kindergarten Activities

- ❑ Model writing throughout the day and have materials available for those children who wish to experiment or play with print.
- ❑ Hang labeled pictures, poetry posters, and the repeated parts of familiar stories in the classroom.
- ❑ As the posters or charts are used with the children, track the words for all children to see. Let the children, if they wish, take pointers and track the memorized words, but do not require them to do so.
- ❑ Manipulate language in the pocket chart as poetry and rhymes are built word-by-word for the children. Have word cards of memorized language available for the children to *play with* as they attempt to put written language together.
- ❑ Have children work with their own names on cards. They can learn to write their names, use their name cards in graphing and counting, explore whose name has a particular letter in it, and invent many other name card activities.

- Have the children sort other picture and word cards. (These can be obtained from the first- and second-grade classrooms when the children have finished a particular theme.) Children play with the cards, learning much about printed language. They sort the cards as to how the words begin, how many letters a word has, whether the word has a particular letter in it, and any number of inventive ways.

At the end of kindergarten we want children to know intuitively, or be on their way to knowing, that language has three characteristics.

- Language is used to express ideas, meanings, and concepts, and to label things, and so on.
- Language has many forms, one of which is print.
- Language is used purposely, usually to record or communicate ideas.

We do not test this or have children try to state it, but after a full year of immersion in oral language, most children have come to understand enough about language to begin formal teaching to learn *how print works* as they become literate.

Notes

The First Weeks of Grade One 3

In order to work with print, children must have an oral language base. If, in grade one, you have children who have had neither the benefit of a literacy nurturing home environment nor a kindergarten experience that allowed them to attain some degree of phonemic awareness, your job will be a challenging one. You will need to follow the curriculum, maintain classroom order with many levels of interest/aptitude, and, most important, work toward bringing your untaught, disadvantaged students up to a working level of preparedness for learning. It will be useful at this time to review pages vii–viii.

Readiness for Writing: Oral Language Time

Oral language time has two purposes:

1. to teach a background of knowledge and vocabulary that will help children read and write about *content*: a particular subject or theme being studied.

2. to have children practice orally one or more of the writing structures of English using the vocabulary and content of the theme being taught, thus preparing them for successful, largely independent, directed writing activities.

We divide the period (20–40 minutes) in half. We teach during the first half, and in the second half we help children as they practice orally. Sometimes each child recites what she plans to write. Frequently we all chant everyone else's ideas.

For example, if the children are learning about animals, oral language time could include one or more of the following activities, with children asking questions and responding orally:

- reading to the class
- showing and discussing illustrations
- classification activities
- using films or videos
- a directed art lesson

WORD BANKS

This teaching is usually followed by creating a noun word bank, or extending an existing word bank. To create an animal word bank, brainstorm for all the animals children know. List their responses on the chalkboard in categories. Have "class secretaries," or older children borrowed from an upper grade, make two copies of each word. Hang one copy on the wall for reference and oral practice. Keep the other copy of the words for *hands-on activities*. [The hands-on set will need the word on both sides, one side with a beginning capital letter and one side with a beginning lowercase letter.]

The following animal word bank came from the initial brainstorming of a grade 1–2 class.

elephant	puffin	frog	bear
lion	shark	snake	deer
jackal	seal	beaver	cougar
antelope	bass	turtle	wolf
rhinoceros	whale	heron	coyote
cheetah	tuna	trout	
leopard	sea lion	water moccasin	
sparrow	kangaroo	worm	horse
owl	cockatoo	slug	chicken
hawk	kaola	centipede	sheep
robin	wallaby	ant	cow
bluebird		beetle	dog
crow			

WRITING STRUCTURES

In the *practice* half of the oral lesson, have children use the word bank vocabulary within a writing structure. The following is a poetic chant suitable for any beginning writer:

_____ here,

_____ there,

_____, _____ everywhere.

Put the structure of the day in the pocket chart, using blank cards for the spaces to be filled in. Using an animal name from the word bank, model a poem, moving the card from blank space to blank space using the capital form for the first three blanks, while saying :

Elephants here,
Elephants there,
Elephants, elephants everywhere.

Track the structure in the pocket chart as the class repeats the chant. Model three or four poems in this way.

The oral lesson is completed by having each child select a favorite animal from the word bank and chant a poem aloud. When every child has said at least one poem, the class is ready to write.

Lions here.	Crows here.
Lions there.	Crows there.
Lions, lions everywhere.	Crows, crows everywhere.

RESPONSE WRITING

During the first two months of school, children might write in response to some of the following frame sentences that have been discussed and recorded during oral language time.

I like _____.	I can't _____.
I like to _____.	A dog can _____.
I have _____.	A cat can _____.
I have one _____.	A fish can _____.
I have two _____.	A dog can't _____.
I have to _____.	A cat can't _____.
I want _____.	A dragon can't _____.
I want to	My _____ is _____.
I can run to _____.	My _____ has _____.
I can run from _____.	My _____ can _____.
I can run around _____.	I play _____.
I can run past _____.	I play in _____.
I can _____.	I play on _____.

And simple rhymes such as:

_____ here,	Here's a _____.
_____ there,	There's a _____.
_____, _____ everywhere.	Everywhere a _____, _____.

One _____,
Two _____,
One, two, three _____.

I like _____,	I love _____,
I like _____,	I love _____,
I like _____,	I love _____,
But I don't like _____.	But I love _____ the best!

I'm afraid of _____,
I'm afraid of _____,
I'm afraid of _____,
But I'm not afraid of _____.

STORY FRAMES

Use the following frame along with reading *Rosie's Walk* by Pat Hutchins to the children.

My [*imaginary or real pet/pet's name*] went for a walk,
around the _____,
under the _____,
past the _____,
over the _____,
and came back when I called.

Write a short story:

This is a _____.   Here is _____.

It has _____.   She (or He) has _____.

It can _____.   She (or He) can _____.

I _____.   I _____.

Readiness for Spelling

Spelling is a skill. Like all skills it requires a little bit of teaching and great deal of practice. We recommend daily, short, snappy, five-minute spelling dictation lessons.

For spelling lessons, the children write on small chalkboards. They sit on the floor or at a table in a group. Each child has a chalkboard, chalk, and a sock for an eraser (use worn-out socks the students bring from home). Children seem to love chalkboards. Writing with chalk on a chalkboard is kinesthetic; children can feel the letters as they write and correct spelling mistakes or poor letter formations easily. We prefer 12" x 18" (30 cm x 45 cm) blank chalkboards and recommend children use them throughout the first year. They are small enough to be portable, but large enough for writing sentences when we do that kind of dictation.

In the first month of first grade, before students learn how to work independently, spelling is taught to the whole class.

In the first few lessons with the entire group

1. Show the students where the chalkboards and socks are kept and have each child pick up one of each.

2. Have the children sit on the floor in groups of four or five, arranged in semi-circles, so that they can look at you and also at each other.

3. Teach the children to hold the chalk, how to put the sock eraser on their nonwriting hand, how to use it, and how to clean the chalkboards and put everything away when finished.

4. Teach at least the first six letters, one at a time, to the whole group. Watch responses and abilities carefully, so that later you can put the children into small ability groups for spelling lessons.

ABILITY GROUPS

Some students enter school almost knowing how print works, while other students know nothing at all about print. Because of these differences and because the teaching of spelling is the teaching of how print works, it is impossible to effectively teach the whole class together. Although we avoid ability grouping for most teaching, twenty years of trial and error have shown us that to teach spelling effectively, children must be taught directly at their levels of understanding. If we do not, our low children never learn, and our top children are not challenged to work at their best ability.

How We Teach Spelling

We begin to teach spelling as soon as possible in grade one, teaching six consonants, *m, s, f, t, b,* and *c,* before we teach a vowel. We teach consonants first because they can be felt within the mouth. Consonants are kinesthetic. Vowels are lost within the mouth, and are erratic in the ways in which they are spelled, making them much more difficult for children to learn.

LESSON ONE: TEACHING THE FIRST CONSONANT

We teach the letters one at a time. The first lesson is designed to help children understand the relationship between speech and print: *when you say a sound you write a letter.* We teach four things at the same time:

1. the name of the letter
2. the way the letter is written
3. the sound the letter represents or *stands for*[1]
4. what we do with our mouth to form the sound

For example, to teach m:

1. Say the letter name, m (em).
2. Write the letter m on the chalkboard while saying the name m.
3. Have the children say the name while writing the letter in the air as you write the letter again on the chalkboard.
4. Have the children write the letter on their individual chalkboards, saying the name as they form the letter. Help as necessary. Have them print m several times, building the association between the name and the letter.
5. Have the children say m again, *holding on to* the sound, creating /m/, the sound m stands for as they speak. Again have the children write the letter m on their chalkboards, saying the sound /m/ as they write the letter.

1. We can discern no completely correct way to teach the consonants. The name itself describes the dilemma: *con* meaning *with* and *sonant* from the root *sonus* meaning *sound*. A consonant to be voiced must be accompanied by a vowel sound. We add the neutral vowel sound, the /uh/, to many of the consonants; thus b becomes /buh/, and t becomes /tuh/. This is a temporary device to get children to begin to understand enough phonics so that they can begin to write; the sounds are used immediately as children learn to put letters together to form words.

6. Ask the children to describe what they do with their mouths to make the sound /m/. (It is inappropriate to teach the terminology of the speech professionals, so get the children's own words to describe the feeling.)

We have found that many children cannot discriminate well enough to *hear* sound likenesses, but that almost all children can learn when the emphasis is upon *the feeling* within the mouth.

LESSON TWO: SEQUENCING

The second lesson is designed to teach children how to use the letter they have learned, how to sequence the letter within a word. To get ready for the lesson, children make their chalkboards into four *Game Boards* by dividing the chalkboard into four equal parts. Then have them draw two short lines in each Game Board.

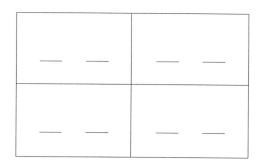

We teach the children which Game Board is number one, two, and so on and have them number the Boards. We tell them that the game we are playing on our chalkboards has one rule: they must say the word after the teacher. Repeating the word is mandatory as they must learn to spell their own speech, and the physical act of saying the word helps many children feel the letter, and locate its position within a word. Children repeat the word as many times as they need to after the teacher pronounces it.

To teach children to sequence the letter m:

1. Say the word *marvelous.*
2. Have the children repeat the word.
3. Ask, "Where did you put your lips together, at the beginning of the word, or at the end?" As you say this, point to the first line in Game Board 1, indicating the line for the initial sound, then to the second line in Game Board 1, indicating the space for the final sound.
4. Let the children repeat the word as often as necessary before deciding their answer.
5. Children indicate the /m/ by writing an m on the first line in Game Board 1.

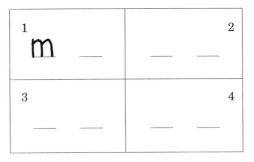

Next dictate a word, perhaps *jam.* Have the children repeat the word. Again ask, "Where did you put your lips together? At the beginning or at the end of the word?" and point to the lines in Game Board 2 that indicate the initial and final positions. Then dictate two more words, perhaps *telegram* and *monster,* to complete the lesson.

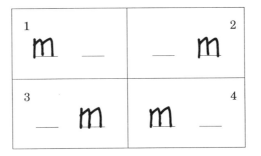

Throughout the lesson watch closely as the children write on their chalkboards, nagging to get the handwriting to a good standard and correcting errors as immediately as possible.

You will make it easy for children by stressing the physical act of saying the word. Don't ask "What do you *hear?*"; instead ask "What did you *say?*" *Children should go from speech to print.*

SPELLING DICTATION ON SUBSEQUENT DAYS

On subsequent days, do similar lessons, introducing an additional letter every second day. During the Game Board sequencing lessons, have the children use as many letters as have been taught. For example, on day three introduce *s* as the second letter. As on day one, teach the *s* lesson to help the children understand the relationship between the sound /s/ and the letter *s*.

On day four, teach the children how to sequence the letter *s* and combine *s* with the letter *m*. For example you might dictate the word *mess*. As children repeat the word ask, "What did you do with your mouth at the beginning of the word? What letter is that?" Children print *m* on the first space in Game Board 1. Have the children repeat the word *mess,* and ask, "What did you do with your mouth at the end of the word? What letter is that?" Children print *s* on the last space of Game Board 1. You might complete the lesson with *milks, slam,* and *stem*.

1 m s	m s 2
3 s m	s m 4

On day five, introduce the letter f, repeating the lesson to help children understand that when you say the sound /f/, you write the letter f. Day six would involve children using the letter f in combination with m and s. We might dictate such words as *stuff*, *farm*, *muff*, and *floss*.

On day seven, introduce another letter, and on day eight have the children use that letter in conjunction with the letters already learned. Continue on until the first six consonants have been taught.

TEACHING THE FIRST VOWEL

Now it's time to teach a vowel so that the children can write whole words. We begin with short vowels so that we can maintain the one-to-one relationship between what we say and what we write. We teach short a as the first vowel. Vowels present a peculiar problem because we cannot feel how we form them within the mouth. We seem to simply open our mouths and the vowel sound comes out. When we ask children what they do with their mouths to form /a/, the most common answer is, "Nothing." We need to make children aware that when we open our mouths and say /a/, this sound is represented by the letter a.

As with the consonants, to introduce a, /a/, teach:

- the name of the letter
- the way to write the letter
- the sound it represents
- what we do with our mouth when we say /a/

WHOLE WORDS

Now combine short a with m, s, f, b, t, and c to have the children write words. Have them divide their chalkboards into four Game Boards without any short lines. Tell them that every word in today's lesson will have a short a in it, and that they can now spell the whole word. Have them say the word as many times as necessary as they spell the whole word; *do not to let them elongate or distort the word in any way.*

For each lesson dictate at least four words. The following might be used in four consecutive lessons:

☑ bat	tam	at	cab
☐ cast	stab	bats	sat
☐ Sam	mat	mast	act
☐ tab	fast	tact	fact

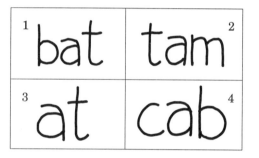

Now that the children have learned a vowel sound and are writing complete words correctly, have them erase their boards as follows:

1. Ask one child which of the four words to erase first, making sure every child in the group finds the word before all erase.

2. Ask another child which word to erase next, and so on, assisting them as necessary.

Saying the words one at a time helps the children to re-identify the word. This method is used when the children cannot yet read the words they have spelled.

Notes

Learning and Practicing 4

When the initial whole class spelling lessons are completed, and children know how to work independently at other tasks, we teach spelling dictation lessons to small groups of children for five minutes each day. Then we send the spelling lesson group on to writing while we circulate, nagging and commenting about the content of the writing the class has already done. We do this for five minutes or so then take another small ability group and teach them for five minutes. We intersperse gentle nagging or reacting to the children's writing with teaching activities throughout the day.

Spelling is practiced throughout the day, any time a child writes. And, *if children are to learn how to spell, they must do their own spelling.* After the first three or four months in first grade, teachers must not spell for them. When children spell they practice phonics. Since we will not spell words correctly for them, children are forced to spell as well as they can, helping themselves to internalize how print works. Their writing shows what they have learned and what they need to be taught next.

Children's daily writings become portfolios for evaluation, and we strongly recommend that they write in bound exercise books so that both the child and the parents can be aware of progress. Individual bound books avoid the problem of having to make copies of the children's writing to create a portfolio.

In the primary grades, we rarely have children rewrite or edit their writings. We have them sit in heterogeneous groups at tables and, through natural sharing, they help each other improve their writing. This, plus our nagging as we circulate while they are writing, is sufficient polishing for beginning writers. Beginners need much more practice than polish, but they also need nagging to help them practice the spelling skills that have been taught.

As children begin to write prolifically, we nag to get only the most annoying mistakes corrected because we cannot catch all the errors. Besides, young children who have to correct every error soon begin to write short, non-imaginative stories.

The Suggested Teaching Sequence

Although *Spelling Through Phonics* is written in a suggested sequence, you may create sequences that suit your children, rather than follow exactly the sequence presented in this book. You must also note each child's most persistent or annoying spelling errors, and teach to eliminate them.

In grade one, after teaching six consonants and a short vowel, usually *a,* teach:

- ❑ another six consonants
- ❑ another short vowel, usually *o*
- ❑ *s* as a plural pattern, whether pronounced /s/ or /z/
- ❑ another six consonants
- ❑ another short vowel, *i*

- the remaining consonants, except x and q
- the short vowel u
- the use of x and qu as representing two sounds
- the short vowel e
- the endings s, *ing*, y, and *er*

When teaching small ability groups, watch the students as they write throughout the day. When they use words correctly in independent writing, it shows that they have learned what you have taught in spelling dictation. Remember, though, that progress will be very different amongst the children.

During the first month, have the class brainstorm and record ideas during the daily oral lessons. Use these ideas for writing structures. (See page 21.) In this writing, the frame part of the structure (for example, "I can _____.") is usually copied correctly. Then the children refer to the brainstormed list on the chalkboard to complete the frame correctly. As children continue oral work and daily spelling lessons they begin to learn the sound/symbol connection; then they no longer want to copy from the chalkboard, but want to try spelling on their own. Encourage this and even demand it. Tell the children to write as much of the words as they can, and teach them how to do this. Remember that at this stage they are practicing the phonics they have learned.

Temporary Spelling

As children practice spelling every day as they write, they spell as well as they can. In so doing, they reinvent alphabetic spelling. This has been termed *inventive spelling*: when children put letters together to form words as well as their knowledge of phonics allows them. We prefer the term *temporary spelling* to describe their initial spellings rather than *inventive*. *Temporary* implies a rudimentary, beginning stage that will change as the child is taught more, and that will lead to standard spelling. It acknowledges that children have not yet learned enough about how letters and print work to spell in standard form. They need to be taught quickly and efficiently so their spelling becomes more nearly standard and, finally, "correct." (Some parents need to be reassured about "uncorrected spelling mistakes." A reproducible form letter to parents explaining temporary spelling is on page 181.)

HOW IT WORKS

Tell children that if they only know the beginning sound to write that letter, and draw a line to show they don't know the rest of the word. If they wanted to write *temper tantrum*, for instance, and could only feel the *t* at the beginning of each word, they would write:

t_____ t_____

If they could feel the letters at the end of the words as well, they would write:

t_____r t_____m

If they can feel letters in the middle of the word, they would write:

tmpr tntrm

Often, children's initial spellings are without vowels, but, as they are taught, they become aware of vowels and add them to words. Then they are able to write *temper tantrum*. The children's independent spelling should gradually reflect what has been taught, although children often use letters and patterns not yet taught. This shouldn't surprise us, as children learn things in many different ways.

Teaching to Eliminate Errors

We frequently group four to eight children for specific instruction designed to eliminate some error. For example, we might discover several children spelling such words as *sandy*, *lucky*, and *candy* as *sande*, *luke*, and *cande*, indicating that they are discriminating the long *e* sound. They are ready to be taught the pattern of long /e/ represented by the letter *y*. If we withhold the teaching, they are likely to practice their nonstandard spelling so often that by the time we teach this common pattern, they will have to unlearn a habit. The ablest children begin to generalize very early, and begin to write freely, using letters that have not been taught. They spell quickly and they spell phonetically with ease, indicating that they have grasped the basic alphabetic notion of letters representing sounds in a left-to-right print sequence.

Teaching At-Risk Children

Some children struggle, not able to grasp the alphabetic notion. Their writing is full of errors and sometimes unintelligible. Usually these are children who have come to school knowing nothing about print. They lack the four to five years of informal language teaching that the child from an environment that emphasized print and literacy has had.

Written language is a puzzle for beginners. Our teaching must make it easy enough to be solved. Sometimes, teachers try to help at-risk children learn by going slower, taking much more time with each letter than they do with the ablest children. But this is neither a good use of time nor beneficial to the children. There are twenty-six letters representing over forty sounds in the puzzle of printed language. Children cannot solve the puzzle— learn how print works—with just one or two letters, no matter how well they know those letters.

Our previously untaught children need to be taught fifteen to twenty letters quickly. We must teach a new letter every second day, showing how to use and sequence them, even though we know that the children aren't understanding our lessons. They cannot begin to understand—to "get it"—until they have enough letters to begin to get a glimmer of how the puzzle of written language works. We must have faith that they will put the puzzle together when we have taught them enough. After all, we talk to our babies for a year, putting language in, before they begin to talk, showing us that they have learned what we have taught.

We have found that the at-risk children usually begin to understand after three or four months of teaching. We then go back and reteach as necessary to make them secure in their learning. It is essential to teach daily and demand that the children "write" daily, even though their writing involves mostly copying and frame sentence work. Children must explore the mysteries of print in every way possible, so we teach how print works in reading activities, writing activities, and spelling activities.

Independent Writing

When we teach children how to write—how to put letters together to form words, and how to put words together to create a variety of structures—we empower them. We make it possible for them to write independently.

We need to teach children before we ask them to practice. Unless we teach "how to" skills directly, many children waste years trying to discover them.

Writing independently should mean what it says: the children write without help. If some children ask for help, saying, "I don't know what to write," or asking, "How do you spell....?", this indicates those children are not ready to practice independent writing.

It is important to realize that independent writing is a practice time wherein children show us what they know about print. If we ask for independent writing before children know enough about print, many of their attempts at writing will result in frustration and failure. The children's egos will suffer just as adults egos suffer when they are told to do something that they cannot do, and then are corrected after they have tried. Discipline and classroom management become problems when children are asked to practice what they don't know. However, when we teach children how and what to write before expecting them to practice, their writing is mostly successful, and they can become truly independent.

TEACHING *WHAT* TO WRITE

Children need to know what to write and they need the concepts and vocabulary necessary to accomplish this task. All areas of the curriculum provide content for writing activities: science and health, social studies, literature, and even mathematics.

These areas provide the subject matter *through which* we teach the skills of writing (and reading, of course). A theme, a unit, or an area of the curriculum provides the content that allows us to teach both subject and skills. This may be done by:

- reading to the children
- showing films and videos
- assigning classification activities
- doing experiments
- art activities
- drama
- going on field trips
- other child-centered activities

The most potent result of all these activities is the opportunity to build up the children's inventory of language. *Word banks* are developed to build the vocabulary required by the children to think, to learn, to read further, to write about the subject, and to write independently. Content and related vocabulary give children what they need in order to write.

TEACHING *HOW* TO WRITE

Children need to know how to write, how to spell, and how to write the structures of the English language. Their spelling does not need to be *standard* in the very early years (see Temporary Spelling, page 35), but children need the ability to spell well enough so that they can write words with ease, and so that others can read what they have written. To write the structures of the English language, children need to be taught how to put words together to write:

- ❏ lists
- ❏ sentences
- ❏ poetic structures
- ❏ connected text, paragraphs, stories, and so on

Why Children Must Write Every Day

We need to have children write independently every day so that we can monitor progress. We circulate as children are writing to help them apply what has been taught. This is individualized teaching and individualized learning. Young children need to be nagged to apply what is being taught. Nagging while children are writing helps children learn what has been taught. Correcting a paper after it is finished wastes teacher time and the corrections are often meaningless to the children. Having children redo work—dragging them back to yesterday—runs counter to the thrust of progress children need at the beginning stages of writing.

Children must write every day for the following reasons.

- to practice what has been taught
- to learn to apply the language skills that have been taught
- to provide a portfolio record of their growth in language skills
- to free time for the teacher to teach small groups of children
- to encourage sharing, cooperative learning, and the development of oral language skills as they sit in small groups to write
- to increase their understanding of the phonics of English, as they apply their how-to-spell skills to unknown words

THREE WRITING ASSIGNMENTS

Children usually have three writing assignments each day. The assignments are written in bound books suitable for beginning writers. Keeping a day-by-day record enables the students to see their own progress, which develops a sense of pride and self-confidence.

1. Directed Writing (The Language Book)

Children write the structure they have practiced orally during oral language time. They write three or four examples if the structure is short. They may illustrate their writing if they choose. The directed writing book shows what has been taught to the child. As examples, see the reproductions of six dated pages from a typical grade-one writing book on page 43, beginning with the first three entries shortly after the start of school and ending in March. Three January samples from a grade-one class illustrate the different ability levels of the children (see page 44).

2. Handwriting

In the first half of grade one, handwriting is assigned daily as children practice the formation of letters they are learning in spelling and phonics. Later, handwriting might not be daily, but assigned as needed.

3. Free Writing (The Journal)

Children keep a journal and write anything they wish in it. This is done almost every day, except at the beginning of grade one. The journal is a test, showing what the child has learned of written language. Usually it is of lesser quality than their directed writing. In some grade-one classes we do not start the journal until the fourth or fifth month of school when the handwriting book is phased out. By then the children have learned enough to write freely and are able to begin writing journals successfully. By grade two, the children's confidence and sense of accomplishment are clearly visible. (See page 45.)

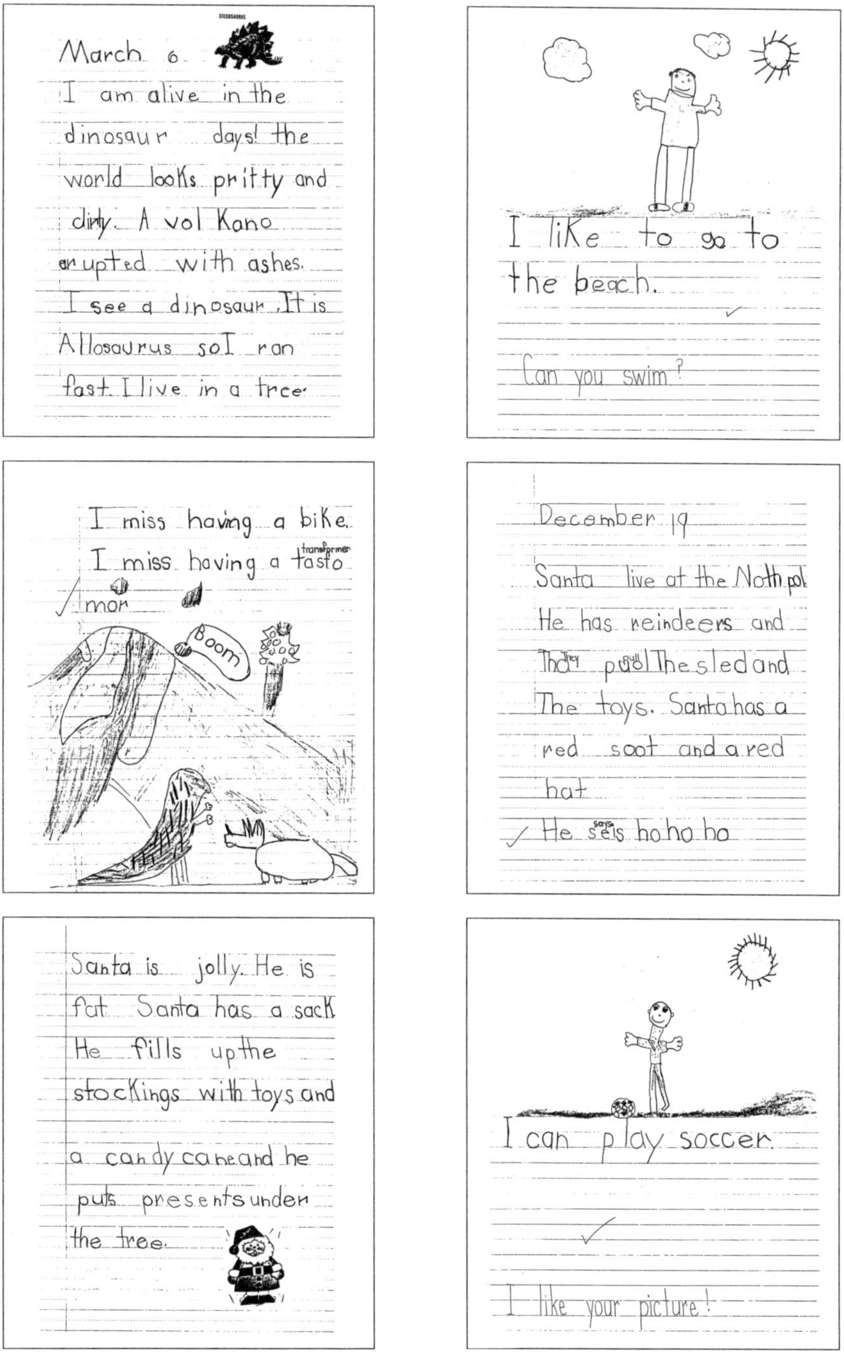

Samples of a grade-one child's writing

Writing samples from four grade-one children taken in January

September 3 ☺
Say goodbye to picnic in the park
say hello to lunch at
school. Say good-bye to
holidays, say hello to
good old school. Say good-
bye to swimming in the
pond, say good-bye to
bloobearys. Say hello

berries
to blak bearys.
Say good bye to Grade1
Say hello to Grade 2.
September 4 1986
My name is Chris. I'm
7 years old. I live on
56 av. I have three brothers
and one sister. One cat to
dog nine birds and six

Jan. 14
Chris and the no good
very bad day.
One day I woke up and
when I had my shower
there was no presher.
And when I had my
toast it was brnt and
the jam was rotan.
When I made my

lunch the bread was
stale. When I went to
school I slid in
the dich. I coud
tell it was going to
be a terrible, horrible,
no good, very bad day.
When I got to school
I was late and it

was the tenth time in
a row so I got sispen-
ed. And when I got
home I got sispened
for a month! Then
I got sent to my room
and stepped on a tack.
I could tell it was
going to be a

terrible, horrible no
good very bad day.
So I went to bed
but how can you
sleep if you cant
sleep? Oooow. It was
a terrible horrible very
bad day!
This is a super story.
I hope you never have a day like this one!

Samples from a grade-two student's journal

Notes

Reacting to Children's Writing 5

Children write to record ideas, to send messages, to remember what they are thinking, or to record what they have learned. They write for dozens of reasons, but rarely are they cognizant that they are writing to learn to write. They are focused upon the content, while we, as teachers, are focused upon the teaching of writing skills *through the content.*

Reacting to Content

What a child writes is of prime importance. We review each child's daily writing and like to react personally in writing. We comment or ask a question to show that we have read and enjoyed the content and to extend a child's thinking. When children are just beginning to write, it is sometimes difficult to respond because they are able to write only a simple three or four word sentence. Regardless, we try to respond. If the child has written "My pet is a cat," we might respond in one of the following ways:

My pet is a dog.

My pet is a cat, too.

My cat's name is Misty.

I wish I had a cat for a pet.

What is your cat's name?

We respond to the content, but we avoid judicial comments of all types. Comments such as "very good" or "try to write more tomorrow" rarely help the child to improve or mature. The best compliment—and the most encouragement—you can give is to respond meaningfully to whatever the child has written.

We try to respond in writing every day because having a response is so important to children. [I can still see the eager looks on the faces of my first-grade children racing to get their books to see what I had written. It was the most important part of their morning. Sometimes they would sit right down and write a comment back. It created a personal bond between my pupils and me. *M.J.M.*]

Reacting to Skill Level

To correct or not to correct, that is the question. Teachers have argued about this for many years. Some teachers—and parents—believe every word should be edited and corrected, while others believe that children should be allowed to be *creative* and spell as well as they are able. What is the answer?

In most school assignments we ask children to practice what we have taught them. For example, when we teach mathematics, we may begin with teaching children how to add. When we ask them to practice math, we give them addition questions of a difficulty level they can handle and they do not normally initiate more complicated tasks. But in spelling, we teach six consonants and a vowel, and ask the children to write every day. The children practice what they've learned but they also want to write wonderful words such as *gorgeous* and *beautiful*!

When children write daily, they frequently want to spell words requiring knowledge well beyond what they have been taught. Writing *grjs* or *gorjus* allows them to practice the phonics they have been taught so far. If we tell them the correct spelling and they copy *gorgeous,* this allows them to practice copying only; they neither practice phonics, nor learn *how* to spell. If we want them to learn to spell we must allow them to practice what they have been taught, which means that, in the beginning, many of their spellings will not be standard. Their use of temporary or inventive spellings allows them to practice what they have learned and shows what they need to be taught. (And we needn't fear that they will somehow get addicted to the wrong spellings; when youngsters start to speak, everyone accepts temporary pronunciation. How many adults do you know who still say wawa for water?)

How to Correct Children's Spelling

That said, children's spelling does need correction by the teacher. The writing they do every day demonstrates their development and growth in applying phonetic skills and spelling principles. When we respond to the skill levels we see in their writing, we need to have two basic spelling lists in mind: (1) words that should be corrected and (2) words that are beyond the child's ability.

1. WORDS THAT SHOULD BE CORRECTED

Children often need a little reminding to help them apply what has been taught to them. When a child misspells a word that should be spelled correctly, we try to catch the word as the child is writing. As we circulate among the students, reading and commenting on their writings, we show them errors and have them correct their work immediately. We don't circle the error with a red pen or make any kind of mark; we just point to the error and have the child correct it. If the child needs help to correct the error, it shows us, as teachers, that the child isn't sure enough about what we have taught; perhaps we need to reteach or review. Of course, we don't point out every correctable mistake. We don't have time to do that, nor do we need to. We have children correct enough of their work so that they learn to apply what has been taught. We don't need to overdo the correcting. A small amount of nagging teaches them to take care and apply what has been taught. We nag and they correct; we nag the mistakes that will make the greatest difference in the child's spelling performance.

When language time is finished, we do no further correcting in the beginning grades. When young children are finished, they are finished, having learned all they can through that day's writing. They don't want to edit or redo work; nor should they. They do want to look for a teacher's comment and they sometimes just reread their pages or the pages of a friend.

2. WORDS THAT ARE BEYOND THE CHILD'S ABILITY

In the first month or so of the formal teaching of phonics, children might learn how to apply five or six consonants. Suddenly they want to spell the word *gorgeous*. They don't know any vowels, but they understand the one-to-one relationship between letters and sounds, and they understand that sounds must be written in a sequence. Applying this knowledge allows them to spell *grjs*, using every phonetic spelling skill they have been taught. If teachers circle words like *grjs* or ask that *grjs* be corrected, they are asking children to do the impossible. At this stage, they do not know enough to write the word in the standard manner. They have written the word as well as possible at their stage of spelling development. It is best to leave such spellings alone, but note what the children have learned and what they need to be taught. Children at the stage of writing *grjs* show that they need to have some vowels taught. Once children understand both consonants and vowels, they need to apply both when writing. Thus, *grjs* would no longer be acceptable. We would nag them into using vowels, and the word might be spelled *gorjus*, still not standard spelling, but a big improvement. Teachers must demand that children apply what has been taught to them; thus all the words that they write should reflect our teaching.

Doozers

Unfortunately, there are words for which there seem to be no phonetic rhyme or reason. Usually, they are words of high frequency usage. Words such as:

they	of	is	are	were
does	you	one	once	was
have	come	said	because	

A long time ago in one of my first grade classes, we were trying to learn how to spell one of these words when a little boy said, "That's a doozer, Mrs. McCracken." The word *doozer* has stuck through the years as it seems appropriate to describe these spelling demons.

After the first four or five months in first grade, when most of the children understand the alphabetic principle of spelling, we can introduce five doozers. Other doozers are introduced at the beginning of grades two and three. Five doozers seem to be enough for both children and teachers to remember at one time throughout the primary grades. *Does, said, they, are,* and *was* are five good doozers for beginning any primary grade.

We place these words on large cards and suggest that they be hung in one or two places in the classroom. As we introduce doozers to children, we make sure that all of them know what the words are. We then ask children to make certain that they copy the doozers correctly whenever they use them in their daily writing. We know of no way to have children learn these words other than by plain, old rote. If we allow children to write *thay* for one or two years, they will practice *thay* several hundred times, making it verydifficult to unlearn.

Five doozers hang in this second-grade classroom; the words are printed on both sides of the cards. There are five similar sets hanging in the classroom so that they are easily seen from anywhere in the room.

Keep an eye on the performance of doozers in your children's writing and, when no mistake has been noted in one particular doozer for two or three weeks, that doozer can be taken from the list and replaced with a doozer the children suggest. Children know the words that give them the most trouble. We run five doozers at a time, and nag or remind children to spell them correctly in their daily writing until the standard spelling is automatic.

Suggested Day Plan to Fit Skill Teaching Into a Full Day

We need large blocks of time so that we can teach children and give them sufficient time to learn and practice what has been taught. What children have been taught is applied throughout the day. Of course, any suggested day plans and time allotments are subject to variation according to school district requirements.

A GENERIC TIMETABLE

Opening Exercises

Mathematics (for whatever time is required by your district)

Oral Language Time (usually whole class teaching for 20 to 40 minutes)

Writing Activity Time
1. Directed writing
2. Free writing
3. Handwriting

During this time take out groups of children for:

❑ small group teaching of spelling (with nagging between groups)

❑ mixed ability groups to teach reading (nagging again)

Sharing Time (at the end of the morning)

Musical Activities (throughout the day)

LUNCH

Quiet Time (read to children, follow-up with practice reading time)

Finish-up Time for Language/Reading/Writing Activities

Curriculum Content (The teaching of content with art, drama, experiments, and other oral or hands-on activities may be specific or form the subject matter for language arts activities.)

Physical Education or Movement Education (needs to be fitted in to meet classroom or school requirements)

Notes

Spelling Dictation Grades 1-3   6

Except at the beginning stages, a typical spelling lesson takes about five minutes. (Review pages 25–31.) For most of the dictation we have provided words in groups of eight, ten, or twelve words arranged left to right. Of course, you may pick and choose as you wish and regional accents—a tendency to drop the r, nonstandard vowel pronunciations, and so on—should be taken into account.

As you introduce each letter, teach (1) its name, (2) how to write it, (3) the sound the letter represents, and (4) what we do with our mouth to form the sound. Have the children prepare their chalkboards, then teach and dictate words for about five minutes. Initially, children write only the beginning and/or ending letters; later they write whole words or as much of each word as they can.

In this book we have not tried to teach every sound or every spelling pattern. We have taught consonants, vowels, and many spelling patterns. If you are required to teach additional letters or patterns (*ph* to represent /f/, for example), the directions we have given for teaching and dictation may be used with lists of words you create.

Teaching Strategies

INTRODUCING

- teach the name of the letter
- teach the sound it makes
- teach how the sound is formed in the mouth
- teach how to print it in lowercase
- teach how to print it in uppercase (or capital)
- have the children say the word and print the letter where they hear it—at the beginning or the end of the word. As more letters are learned, have the children print both initial and final letters.

PRACTICING

Have the children say each word after you and print the letters for the sounds they say. These will progress from only the initial or final letter, to both, then to medial consonants as well, finally to whole words.

REVIEWING

Follow the directions for each review. Reviews become more difficult as more letters are added, but the number of words per lesson are reduced. These reviews provide the opportunity to see progress and also to catch errors so that reteaching can occur as necessary.

TEACHING

In grades two and three, when all the letters have been introduced and well practiced, teach specifics as detailed. Most instruction at this stage will focus on spelling patterns, adding endings to change meanings, the use of affixes, and so on. These lists do not cover everything (contractions, for instance). Initiate this teaching as needed.

Grades One to Three Contents

GRADE ONE

GRADE TWO

GRADE THREE

Notes

Grade
Spelling Dictation

Introducing *M*

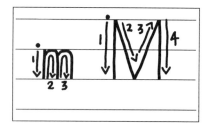

- [ ] monster   tram   Milwaukee   minimum
  macadam   maim   million   material

- [ ] magnificent   mighty   confirm   chum
  ham   mellow   arm   meat

- [ ] clam   mom   multiply   alarm
  mystery   firm   stem   harm

- [ ] inform   mud   mechanism   many
  minute   motor   Maggie   madam

- [ ] mountain   music   medium   medicine
  trim   middle   charm   melody

Introducing *S*

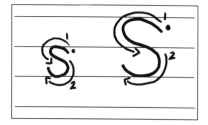

- [ ] seven   sunshine   atlas   sorting
  Sam   bus   support   bakes

- [ ] class   San Diego   second   sifter
  cress   dress   sixteen   seventy

- [ ] sunsets   success   stops   sports
  gorgeous   Christmas   lakes   senior

- [ ] superior   summer   units   stocking
  sis   sudden   gets   sweets

- [ ] sent   supper   cakes   claps
  sofa   fuss   famous   spatter

Practicing *M* and *S*

- [ ] mass   sunbeam   stem   mounts
  slam   marvelous   memories   muss

- [ ] stream   slum   markets   meets
  milks   mishaps   storm   scream

- [ ] seem   scram   solarium   skim
  swim   strum   mistiness   mindless

- [ ] metropolis   mists   moss   microscopes
  miss   steam   mates   Sam

Introducing *F*

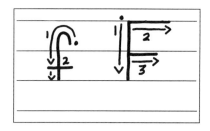

- frontier   frown   calf   cliff
  half   faster   funny   folder

- fluff   father   belief   reef
  if   fifty   further   elf

- off   fling   brief   feast
  factory   gruff   cuff   surf

- huff   grief   loaf   deaf
  puff   forest   relief   finger

- find   freeway   five   friendly
  turf   February   France   yourself

Practicing *M, S,* and *F*

- flakes   stuff   floss   freaks
  muss   form   mischief   molasses

- myself   firm   storm   self
  flutes   film   matters   scream

- farm   scuff   from   Morris
  floats   foam   mastiff   serious

- masks   muff   mysterious   flaps
  Muffett   surf   staff   stream

- mutters   fastens   sheriff   famous
  miff   flasks   miss   stuffs

Introducing *B*

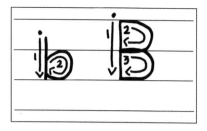

- ☐ bleach   butterfly   bathtub   cub
     scrub   bacon   brainstorm   beetle

- ☐ barb   cob   tub   bulb
     brook   gob   crib   billiard

- ☐ Bob   jab   biscuit   blip
     grub   corncob   throb   bib

- ☐ lab   job   bear   button
     butler   boiling   black   butter

- ☐ crab   drab   battle   blotter
     blurb   better   basket   grab

Practicing *M*, *S*, *F*, and *B*

- ☐ bus   flab   brim   bits
     bass   stiff   sandstorm   barnacles

- ☐ flub   stub   fib   bedlam
     sob   moss   form   broom

- ☐ fabulous   scarf   fiberglass   Birmingham
     scrub   beef   famous   blab

- ☐ marvelous   swab   breaks   backs
     belief   bloom   bottom   scoff

- ☐ Bellingham   stab   bluff   firm
     surpass   boom   bailiff   skim

Introducing *T*

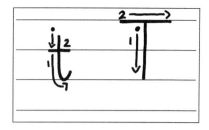

- ☐ right
  tent
- limit
  tender
- today
  jacket
- table
  headlight

- ☐ coat
  town
- tallest
  part
- toast
  transport
- cut
  terrible

- ☐ total
  temper
- travel
  temple
- tension
  cannot
- tight
  train

- ☐ truant
  terminal
- cast
  last
- important
  trucking
- talking
  quit

- ☐ built
  tangent
- dart
  detergent
- trot
  pennant
- permanent
  tenant

Practicing *M, S, F, B,* and *T*

When dictating words such as "forest," "stiff," or "smart" some children may be able to tell you what *two* sounds they say at the beginning, or at the end of the word.

☐ market   term   summit   tennis
    secret   freight   mist   skirt

☐ forest   but   sport   fort
    turf   sit   flashlight   start

☐ best   seat   spirit   tub
    stab   team   fast   fit

☐ flat   sub   blast   simplest
    smart   smurf   smokes   smallest

☐ stylist   flames   forget   stiff
    stem   moist   staff   meats

Introducing *C*

- [ ] plastic   capable   casual   arithmetic
  clothing   Atlantic   coming   combat

- [ ] music   camel   climax   clatter
  conductor   attic   gigantic   elastic

- [ ] curly   crushing   rustic   completion
  Pacific   anemic   creature   drastic

- [ ] canning   closure   hectic   candy
  public   crush   Antarctic   dynamic

- [ ] caustic   classic   carousel   electric
  cursive   panic   havoc   crater

Practicing *M, S, F, B, T,* and *C*

- [ ] mosaic   socket   crabs   carnivals
  cram   tonic   boost   fantastic

- [ ] basic   curb   cutlass   spoof
  bathroom   cannot   sporadic   flotsam

- [ ] bright   carrot   climates   talc
  consonant   mischief   telescopes   flatboat

- [ ] fabric   tasteless   misinform   commandant
  student   blanket   cutlass   monstrous

- [ ] talcum   stiffness   bottom   critic
  toxic   felt   spirit   bouquet

Reviewing what has been taught so far

For this lesson, there should be no lines inside the Game Boards. Tell the children they are to repeat the word for the beginning and ending sounds as they have been doing, but that today's words will also have a sound that they know somewhere in the middle.

Review the names of the six letters taught so far, and put them on the large chalkboard or on your own small chalkboard. *You may only be able to dictate two or three words in a lesson.*

☐ craft	tablet	countess
☐ torment	confess	brightness
☐ crest	cost	moment
☐ buffet	cobweb	magnifies
☐ flames	success	beset
☐ classic	mightiness	straight

If some children seem ready for a special challenge you may wish to work with the following words. All of them have "in the middle" more than one sound the children have learned.

☐ transmit	bombardment	contrast
☐ brontosaurus	monstrous	mysterious
☐ contest	settlement	movements
☐ fantastic	broadcast	crickets
☐ crossarm	substitutes	submarines

Teaching short vowels

Thus far you have taught consonant sounds only, sounds that can be felt in the mouth. Teaching this short vowel now retains the one-to-one relationship between speech and print; when you say a sound you write a letter.

Short a is a good first vowel choice as it has the least dialectic variation throughout North America. Short a can be used at the beginning of a word, and in the middle, but not at the end of a word.

Start, as before, by teaching the four things about the letter: its name: a, its sound: /a/-'ah,' and how to write it. Teach also that short a really doesn't have a "feel" in the mouth, but that vowel sounds must be *heard*.

Introducing short *a*

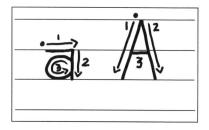

Have the children divide their chalkboards into four Game
Boards. Tell them you are going to say some words and that
the /a/ may be at the beginning or in the middle of the word.
Ask the children to repeat each word after you. If they say
/a/, they should print *a;* if they don't say /a/ they should leave
that Game Board empty.

☐ animal	afloat	late	after
accord	gosh	and	aster
☐ boil	cob	mend	custard
agitate	monster	apple	terrible
☐ anchor	tenth	antenna	antic
acting	appetite	approve	ash
☐ black	angry	form	axe
cast	last	plaster	damp
☐ Atlantic	taxi	antelope	waist
anniversary	admit	dog	dagger

Dictate the following words and have the children write both
the beginning and ending sounds:

☐ Alps	accent	ant	apart
atlas	assistant	atom	aspect
☐ alarm	apparatus	appetites	apes
amiss	at	about	album
☐ admit	advent	acrobat	act
absent	affirm	atom	abbot

Teaching short *a* in medial position

[Remember to say each word only once. The children may say the word as often as necessary. Discourage elongating of sounds.]

Tell the children that they are now going to spell whole words. There should be no lines at all on their chalkboards.

1. Say the word "sat," for example.
2. Have each child repeat the word.
3. Ask, "What did you say *first?*"
4. The children respond, repeating the word as necessary to identify /s/ as *s*.
5. The children write *s* on their chalkboards.
6. Have the children say the word again. (You should say the word only if the children cannot remember it.)
7. Ask, "What did you say *after* the s, after /s/?"
8. Get the children to identify the short /a/ and to write the letter *a* on their chalkboards.
9. Now have the children say the word again, and ask, "What did you say at the *end* of the word?"
10. The children identify the /t/ and write *t* to complete the word.
11. Have everyone point to the whole word and say it.
12. Dictate three more words and have the children write each word on their chalkboard.
13. When all four words have been written on their chalkboards, say one of the words, and have each child point to the word on his or her own chalkboard and read it, and then erase it. Say a second word, have the children point, read, and then erase, and so on until their boards are clean. This reverses the process of writing into reading, a task that some children find difficult.

Spelling whole words after teaching short *a*

For each lesson dictate at least four words.

☐ tab	bat	mat	am
☐ fat	mast	fact	fast
☐ Sam	tact	at	cats
☐ tam	cat	sat	cast
☐ masts	stab	tabs	aft
☐ Mac	act	stabs	mats

[In their free writing the children may spell "ask" as "asc," "staff" as "staf," and so on. Accept these spellings without comment. The children are spelling as well as they have been taught. Correction at this time will only confuse them.]

Introducing *R*

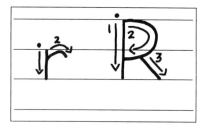

- [ ] robin   reading   war   radar
  ripe   lower   rarer   round

- [ ] rasher   roper   pear   raisin
  roar   romp   air   shower

- [ ] roll   liar   power   chair
  royal   rodeo   car   really

- [ ] appear   rainy   door   wear
  rapid   repair   rustler   runner

- [ ] dear   river   rug   doctor
  jar   poor   aster   roller

Practicing *R* with *M, S, F, B, T,* and *C*

| ❏ tear | rim | right | repeat |
| clear | for | road | clatter |

| ❏ roof | stair | flower | rub |
| relief | motor | rot | redness |

| ❏ bear | riot | clear | root |
| floor | rear | roundness | caterpillar |

| ❏ carrier | relic | fear | fir |
| cashier | blower | center | caller |

You may wish to challenge some of the children to spell the following whole words.

| ❏ rat | ram | raft | crab |

| ❏ cram | tram | tract | scram |

Introducing *L*

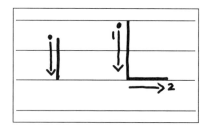

- ☐ land   peel   well   listen
  heal   pail   retail   gill

- ☐ pill   jail   natural   dial
  steal   lettuce   litter   squeal

- ☐ capital   initial   label   leap
  log   deal   metal   shell

- ☐ veil   pal   goal   leg
  like   lead   lovely   later

- ☐ leash   load   latch   lucky
  creel   long   dreadful   legal

Practicing *L* with *M, S, F, B, T, C,* and *R*

As usual, have the children print the initial and final sounds. At this stage they may be able to handle ten words in one dictation.

- ☐ liar   frail   lift   lost   real
  let   coal   spool   soul   light

- ☐ towel   list   feel   sell   sill
  bell   meal   fowl   royal   call

- ☐ metal   fatal   scandal   bowl   fool
  loam   till   bail   ball   tool

- ☐ motel   legal   cool   lab   tell
  sail   lot   lower   leaf   total

Practicing short *a* with *M, S, F, B, T, C, R,* and *L*

Have the children write the following whole words.

☐ slat	flat	scram	rams
☐ slam	lab	flab	lam
☐ flats	crab	brat	rats
☐ tram	clam	mast	fast
☐ cram	blab	slams	stab
☐ last	fact	blast	tram

Introducing *P*

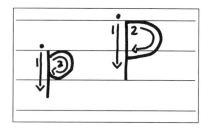

- [ ] deep
  drip

  grip
  yelp

  plod
  penalty

  person
  gallop

- [ ] nap
  limp

  pretty
  thump

  plenty
  lamp

  grasp
  cheap

- [ ] pried
  help

  poke
  prop

  porcupine
  trap

  shrimp
  pup

- [ ] public
  dip

  pig
  dump

  prison
  heap

  purple
  poking

- [ ] primp
  plop

  pretend
  pork

  punk
  chimp

  plump
  purpose

Practicing *P* with *M, S, F, B, T, C, R,* and *L*

Have the children print the first and last letters. [Some children may be able to print the intermediate consonants as well.]

❑ slump	sloop	petal	possum	prior
tip	loop	lump	pear	stop
❑ pop	proof	pail	loop	creep
poem	mop	peat	bump	coop
❑ post	pleat	mumps	fantastic	perfect
flap	reap	top	poet	panic
❑ puff	peril	flop	bottom	prop
plump	cup	clutter	pomp	romp

Reviewing what has been taught so far

Have children print the whole word.

❑ cap	rap	cramp	craft	slaps
❑ past	flap	trap	lamp	laps
❑ spat	camp	tap	slap	slam
❑ stamp	ramp	pat	clamp	pact
❑ lap	fact	pals	map	clasp
❑ strap	rasp	amps	maps	flat
❑ claps	tramp	clamps	last	blast
❑ slat	strap	tamps	rats	tramps

Introducing short *o*

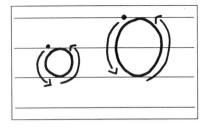

After teaching the short *o* and its /aw/ sound to children, dictate the following words. Have the children write the letters for the initial and final sounds.

☐ octopus   off   optimum   oddness
    object   observant   occasional   omnibus

☐ osmosis   Oscar   offset   operator
    otter   officer   offer   omelet

To introduce short *o* in the medial position, you might like to review page 74. Have the children write the following whole words.

☐ pot	sob	soft	lot	plot
☐ slob	stop	plop	croft	mob
☐ loft	pots	rot	mop	stops
☐ cot	tops	clot	blots	robs
☐ cop	flop	prop	cops	trots
☐ slot	trot	blot	pompom	crops
☐ spot	lots	top	Bob	prom
☐ rob	cob	soft	plops	log

Introducing *D*

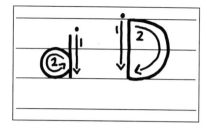

☐ doom	lard	mold	send
mood	dramatic	dead	did
☐ dust	dart	told	distend
card	find	dud	dad
☐ bald	bold	bend	tried
dries	drastic	cord	called
☐ dried	dashed	land	planned
broad	found	detailed	mud
☐ dim	road	read	mend
dear	died	sold	mid

Practicing *D* with short *a* and short *o*

Have the children write the whole word.

☐ drops	pod	pads	lads	rod
☐ dots	ad	dot	scads	glad
☐ bad	sad	dam	clad	dad
☐ mad	dabs	dram	plod	data
☐ trod	lad	drat	fad	clod

Introducing *G*

Have the children write both the beginning and ending sounds.

☐ rug	grub	slug	glitter
garter	gum	gull	gust
☐ gravel	dog	gold	mug
drag	stag	grab	gill
☐ big	pig	brag	grass
gram	catalog	globes	tag
☐ gulf	peg	great	grammar
leg	fog	tug	mug

Practicing *G* with short *a* and short *o*

Have the children write the whole word.

☐ log	brag	bog	gab	drag
☐ gap	grasp	flag	gasp	golf
☐ tag	tog	gag	slag	slog
☐ grab	gal	flag	smog	got
☐ bag	dog	fog	rag	gas
☐ frog	graft	grog	gram	cog

Reviewing what has been taught so far

Children should be able to spell the whole word.

☐ scat	frost	romp	bag	cop
☐ cost	ramp	bog	crop	cramp
☐ tramp	lamp	stamp	pots	soft
☐ atop	sag	last	gas	pact
☐ flag	prom	past	stomp	fact
☐ land	bland	plant	flop	stops

Special challenge words for children who are doing well:

☐ drama   catalog   program   compact   tract

Writing sentences

If children have been writing each day using frame sentences so that they know how to spell *can, like, to, see, have, run,* and so on, dictate a short sentence every other day to practice capitalization, punctuation, and spacing of words.

☐ I can stop.	I like frogs.	I like to see a cat.
☐ I can go fast.	I see a cat.	I have a cat.
☐ My cat is sad.	I can golf.	My cat can stop.

Introducing N

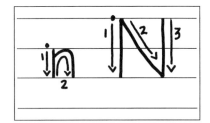

Have the children print the initial and final letters. [Note there are now ten words in a lesson.]

☐ seen	tin	torn	refrain	train
news	fan	fun	green	near
☐ begin	fallen	nest	national	been
neat	sin	bun	darn	town
☐ fin	net	spin	mean	born
teen	blamed	napkin	named	flown

Practicing N with short a and short o

Have the children print the whole word. [Note there are now six words in a lesson.]

☐ man	ant	Stan	land	not	stand
☐ snob	blond	snap	snag	contact	pan
☐ pond	fond	nag	band	sand	can
☐ plant	slant	clan	ran	strap	Don
☐ bond	grand	on	brand	tan	plan
☐ pant	rant	gland	bland	strand	fan

Introducing *W*

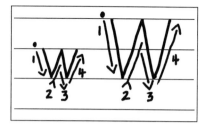

☐ warm   waist   wagon   waif   wit
  west   warp   wood   wafer   win

☐ wait   warf   word   swat   well
  wasp   worst   woolen   want   wed

☐ war   wig   warn   wart   wall
  wool   worm   wag   wolf   web

Challenge words:

☐ swamp   swap   swell   twist   twin

Introducing short *i*

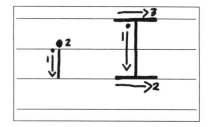

After teaching the vowel's name and sound, dictate the following words. Have the children write the first two letters and the final letter or letters.

☐ imp   imagination   illustration   indeed
    impart   impress   impair   import

☐ important   indent   illegal   independent
    impersonal   inboard   immortal   imperial

Practicing short *i*

Have the children print the whole word.

☐ fit	spit	snip	tilt	twig
☐ sit	flit	rip	sift	twin
☐ wilt	wit	wind	slip	gift
☐ pit	flip	mist	slid	bit
☐ wig	win	swim	silt	swift
☐ lilt	big	slit	rig	pits
☐ dig	spin	lift	slim	list
☐ clip	fist	strip	rim	stilt

Reviewing what has been taught so far

Have the children print the whole word.

❑ fast	drop	wit	sift	fist
❑ slip	mist	crisp	sap	slap
❑ clasp	cost	spot	grand	clop
❑ trip	limp	lost	mint	trap
❑ lamp	last	lint	sprint	tramp
❑ list	spit	plastic	mast	wisp
❑ grin	clip	drip	flat	soft
❑ web	flit	tap	wig	twin

Introducing *H*

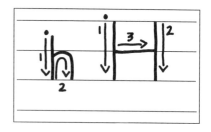

- [ ] hear   Helen   hurt   hurl   harp
     heap   held   havoc   humor   hectic

- [ ] half   hug   Harold   help   hazard
     heel   hamster   hostess   Halloween   hotel

- [ ] hammer   had   harm   haul   hop
     harmless   horn   harp   horrible   habit

Practicing *H* with all known consonants and vowels

Have the children write the whole word.

- [ ] hop   hand   has   had
     hid   hip   hilt   hit

- [ ] ham   hint   hat   him
     hot   hats   his   habit

- [ ] hag   hips   habits   hilts
     hands   hints   hips   hog

Introducing *J*

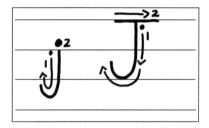

- [ ] joker   jester   jaguar   jackpot
  journal   just   Janet   jail

- [ ] John   jar   jeer   James
  jewel   jump   joint   jargon

- [ ] junior   Jerusalem   Jean   judged
  jackal   Jeep   jacket   Japan

- [ ] jog   jolt   jack   jut
  juror   jig   Jim   jab

Introducing *K*

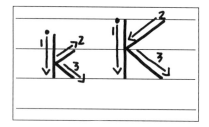

Encourage children to try the medial sounds.

❏ kipper	keg	keen	Karen
kept	kennel	kernel	keep
❏ kerchief	kelp	kilt	kid
kind	kiss	kitten	kink
❏ kidnap	keeper	kinder	kick
kindness	keel	keen	kindergarten

Introducing *V*

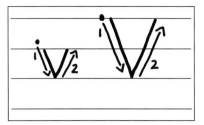

Encourage children to try the medial sounds.

☐ veil	verbal	veal	veer
violet	vault	valiant	vacuum
☐ vertical	veteran	vain	velvet
valid	vacation	vagrant	vapor
☐ Venus	various	volcanic	vast
vacant	violin	vagabond	ventriloquist

Practicing *W, H, J, K,* and *V* with short *a, i,* and *o*

Have the children write the entire word.

☐ jam	vat	van	jag
jog	hilt	vast	job
☐ kilt	twist	hint	hag
wig	wag	wilt	kin
☐ twig	vivid	wink	wisp
hog	wind	jot	jig

Introducing short *u*

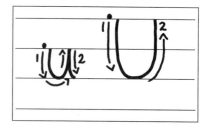

After teaching children the short *u* vowel and its /uh/ sound, dictate the following words, having the children spell at least the initial and final sounds.

☐ under   unravel   unpack   unfair   upturn
  umpteen   untold   unusual   unfed   utter

☐ usher   until   uncoated   unarmed   uphold
  unwrap   unfold   uproot   unfasten   uphill

☐ underarm   undecided   upon   unzip   understand
  untwist   uptown   undercut   upper   underwear

Practicing short *u* in medial position

Have the children write the whole word.

☐ bud   cut   bun   tut   cud   mud

☐ must   rust   dust   cusp   mug   hug

☐ bum   slug   strum   fun   stun   cup

☐ bus   trust   tut   fund   plum   sum

Reviewing what has been taught so far

Have the children write the whole word. Take two or three days to review as many words per day as the children are capable of.

❑ brag	hog	hag	hug	big	bog
❑ bag	bug	hot	hut	rig	gag
❑ rag	flag	rug	gun	gasp	dog
❑ dig	dug	clip	clog	clap	stub
❑ stab	swim	clam	jump	vamp	kit
❑ slum	slim	must	crust	buts	nuts
❑ just	gust	stomp	plump	dump	smug
❑ lump	stump	stamp	hum	gum	lamp
❑ tramp	tuft	runt	stunt	punt	skip
❑ strip	flip	flop	brand	brunt	brim
❑ trim	rim	rum	skit	slop	pop
❑ plop	sip	trap	drip	stand	brand

Introducing *Y*

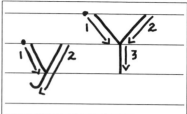

Some children may add medial sounds or write the whole word.

- [ ] yet   yell   yacht   yak   yam   yap
  yard   yank   yarn   yes   year   yeast

- [ ] York   yearn   yodel   yawn   yip   yen
  yolk   yield   yo-yo   yonder   yurt   your

Introducing *Qu*

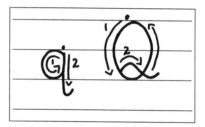

Have the children print *qu* and at least the ending sound that they say. Encourage them to write any sounds that come before the /kw/ sound and the medial vowel even though some are long.

- [ ] quill   quell   queen   quit
  quad   quilt   quite   question

- [ ] request   quiet   quarter   quaint
  quest   quick   quarrel   quiver

- [ ] quintuplet   inquest   quip   queer
  quaver   quail   quart   quake

- [ ] Quaker   equipment   equal   acquaint
  equator   require   quiet   quieter

Introducing Z

Have the children print as much of each word as they are able to.

- [ ] zinc   whiz   jazz   zero   zebra
      zoo   zoom   zeal   zest   zigzag

- [ ] quiz   razz   zany   buzz   zap
      zip   frizz   zipper   zeppelin   zircon

Introducing X

Tell the children that the letter x is rarely used, and that it represents the /ks/ sound, but never at the beginning of a word. Teach the children that *other* letters, *cks* and *ks,* usually represent the /ks/ sound. Encourage them to write as much of each word as possible, using x to represent /ks/.

- [ ] ox   six   sex   box   fix
      vex   pox   tax   fox   mix

- [ ] exit   mix   ax   exam   exhaust
      flax   extra   wax   relax   maximum

Introducing short *e*

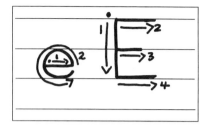

Teach the children the sound, /e/, of the short vowel *e*. Many dialects make little distinction between short *e* and short *i;* acknowledge this as needed. Then dictate the following words. The children should spell the whole word. Review the consonants as needed.

☐ wet	hem	red	mend	met	stem
☐ bed	send	pet	hen	led	fled
☐ lend	get	den	bled	bend	let
☐ glen	sled	tend	net	wed	wend
☐ set	pen	fed	spend	bet	quest
☐ blend	west	tent	weld	nest	went
☐ cleft	elf	best	sent	deft	self
☐ pest	spent	belt	jest	bent	leg
☐ felt	lest	help	peg	keg	welt
☐ test	trend	men	left	pep	pelt

Reviewing consonant sounds, sequencing of sounds, and short vowels

The following words are completely regular. The children should be able to spell all of them. Use the words to review and to determine if any sounds need reteaching.

☐ blab	crisp	stop	crab	bump	gun
☐ brag	grab	skid	plop	bled	frog
☐ pig	nod	mint	sad	rug	self
☐ pond	rob	but	stab	lump	grunt
☐ hid	blimp	fled	dig	rim	brim
☐ sift	glad	plug	soft	mad	blob
☐ raft	belt	kept	twist	crust	print
☐ him	stand	twin	quiz	loft	dad
☐ plod	flint	craft	help	romp	golf
☐ grim	trend	sob	jam	slept	went
☐ mud	hint	rent	sift	fig	web
☐ held	skin	fend	gland	lift	slim
☐ pond	not	blot	bet	glut	blend
☐ if	cab	hog	gulp	hunt	drift

Spelling two-syllable words

Children will now enjoy writing two syllable purely phonetic words. Use the following steps to dictate several groups of words to develop confidence and to review all the letters.

1. Say, "cabin." Have the children repeat, "cabin." Make sure every child says the word.
2. Ask the children to clap the word, "ca-bin." Make sure that the children clap two times indicating that they understand the two syllables.
3. Tell the children to draw two lines on their chalkboards, one for each clap.

4. Ask the children to repeat the word, "cabin," clapping again.
5. Ask, "What did you say with the first clap?"
6. If children respond "cab," have them write it on the first line. (If they respond "ca," have them write *ca* on the first line with *bin* becoming the second syllable.)
7. Next, ask, "What did you say with the second clap?"
8. Children respond and write "in" (or "bin") on the second line.
9. Then have children write the whole word underneath the two syllables.

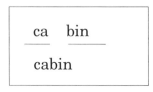

Practicing two-syllable words

Dictate four or five words at a time, as described on page 100. Note that the *re-* and *de-* words given here are pronounced with a short *e* rather than a long *e*.

☐ humbug	prevent	cabin	planet	extent
☐ nutmeg	present	upset	husband	helper
☐ invest	repent	motel	intend	relax
☐ contest	request	repast	frantic	music
☐ revolt	depend	unkind	unwind	exist
☐ conflict	defend	instruct	panic	sedan
☐ habit	credit	inland	resist	exam
☐ implant	decamp	exit	debit	protect
☐ expand	encamp	suspect	contest	invent
☐ exact	satin	antic	cosmic	golden
☐ expend	invest	mishap	April	hotel
☐ replant	plastic	oldest	context	enact

Practicing three- and four-syllable words

Have the children clap and count the number of syllables for the following words, and put the lines required on their chalkboards before they write.

☐ fantastic	tomato	potato
☐ testament	habitat	inhabit
☐ electric	Sacramento	compliment
☐ understand	misunderstand	defender

Adding the endings s, *ing, y,* and *er*

Most children should find adding endings a relatively simple task. Dictate words from each section until children use the ending comfortably.

Adding s to words that require no other change

Teach the children that s is used two ways: as a plural—as in 'cats'—or as a third person verb—as in 'sits.' The sound may be /s/ or /z/.

☐ dusts	hams	cats	bands	crusts
hens	hands	wilts	runs	pigs
☐ bins	stands	jams	lists	fits
hops	dogs	taps	mists	skip
☐ buns	sits	tilts	bits	bets
stubs	rugs	bans	spots	beds
☐ steps	cans	bats	jigs	flags
lasts	sags	dents	posts	pins
☐ flats	pans	strums	blasts	wigs
wets	brats	gabs	bugs	wins
☐ rags	hats	rusts	swats	mugs
swaps	digs	nests	pests	vests
☐ prints	buds	dims	crafts	plugs
rests	figs	rents	bumps	tents
☐ golfs	skins	lamps	rafts	jests
cabs	swims	rests	crabs	skids

Adding *ing* to words that require no other change

- [ ] standing   handing   blinking   sanding
      sending   bending   winking   granting

- [ ] cresting   tending   acting   jumping
      casting   milking   asking   hunting

- [ ] dusting   tinting   basking   bumping
      nesting   blending   tenting   bunting

- [ ] planting   lasting   welding   stinking
      jilting   twisting   mending   minding

- [ ] hinting   clumping   finding   rusting
      flunking   denting   asking   golfing

- [ ] slinking   printing   renting   junking
      slanting   landing   belting   bunking

Using *y* on the end of words

Teach the children that some words use *y* to represent the long /e/ sound (such as *candy*). Other words can be changed from a noun to an adjective by adding *y* (such as *crusty*).

- [ ] crusty   pesky   bumpy   rusty   cranky
      gimpy   sandy   spunky   clumsy   jumpy

- [ ] candy   softy   crispy   grumpy   dusty
      lefty   slinky   flunky   dandy   frisky

- [ ] lumpy   milky   nasty   silky   hefty
      gusty   crafty   sulky   testy   lanky

- [ ] slanty   junky   pinky   springy   sixty
      stumpy   stringy   stinky   lofty   windy

Using *er* on the end of words

If the children are ready for such explanations, tell them that *er* can change a verb to a noun (*help* to *helper*, for example); can change an adjective (from *fast* to *faster*, for example); and is also a common ending for both nouns (such as *fender*) and verbs (such as *pilfer*).

☐ faster   pester   pilfer   helper
  sender   boxer   renter   fluster

☐ fender   gander   planter   stricter
  buster   filter   plunder   milder

☐ tinder   plaster   folder   winter
  master   milker   sander   stomper

☐ crisper   blister   blaster   golfer
  bumper   wilder   blunder   caster

☐ sprinter   older   duster   aster
  after   stamper   under   camper

☐ singer   springer   fonder   spender
  swinger   hinder   bolder   blinder

☐ sister   tender   yonder   mister
  fester   luster   colder   grander

Introducing *ch* in initial and final position

Teach the children that each time they say the /ch/ sound they are to write the two letters *ch*. Children should be able to write the whole word.

- ☐ chest   chub   lunch   much
  belch   chat   chant   bunch

- ☐ bench   branch   chump   clench
  munch   pinch   chap   chimp

- ☐ inch   child   punch   flinch
  clinch   champ   chug   crunch

- ☐ drench   chin   perch   ranch
  rancher   brunch   chip   children

Introducing *sh* in initial and final position

Teach the children that each time they say the /sh/ sound they are to write the two letters, *sh*. Children should be able to write the whole word.

- ☐ shiver   shining   fish   bash
  shag   shaft   flash   dish

- ☐ shed   shop   ash   mash
  shanty   shelf   mesh   hush

- ☐ ship   shoplift   gush   dash
  shelter   shot   gash   crush

- ☐ shut   sham   rush   mush
  shunt   shush   sash   rash

- ☐ swish   hash   splash   lush
  wish   smash   lash   trash

Introducing *th* in initial and final position

Tell the children that each time they feel the /th/ sound they are to write the two letters, *th*.

- ☐ that   theft   both   this   thing
  moth   then   thrift   fifth   than

- ☐ think   bath   them   thinly   filth
  thunder   thrush   tenth   thump   froth

- ☐ thank   math   thin   eleventh   sixth
  with   cloth   seventh   ninth   path

Practicing *ch,* *sh,* and *th*

Dictate these words as needed to review or reintroduce the three digraphs, *ch*, *sh,* and *th.*

ch

☐ chop   children   chimp   chapter   hunch
    chip   chicken   chump   pinch   punch

☐ chug   chin   achoo   inch   bunch
    chum   chant   drench   French   finch

☐ chap   chest   stench   ranch   porch
    charm   much   bench   branch   lunch

☐ champ   such   richly   clinch   crunch
    child   clench   belch   enchant   rich

sh

☐ shut   ash   mash   gush   shark
    ship   slash   rash   refresh   crash

☐ shop   cash   sash   splash   flesh
    shoo   crush   lush   flushing   dash

☐ short   flash   shunt   flush   slush
    shorn   gash   dish   mesh   finish

th

❏ thin	then	gothic	bath	forth
this	throb	northern	math	north
❏ that	thick	bathtub	path	tooth
thus	thank	athlete	ninth	broth
❏ thorn	think	thrash	fifth	cloth
three	thing	pathway	sixth	both

Introducing long vowels in grade one

Until now children may have been spelling long vowels by merely using the single letters. Long vowels can be introduced to first-grade children by introducing the simple spelling pattern of vowel-consonant-*e* for each long vowel sound, as one way to spell the long sound. (Refer to page 143 for the discussion and introduction of long vowels.)

Long *a*

☐ came	mane	gate	take	sale
same	Jane	late	rake	stale
☐ blame	crane	mate	bake	wade
shame	lane	skate	sake	bare
☐ dame	pane	fate	wake	shape
fame	flame	hate	flake	tape
☐ game	tame	plate	shake	stake
lame	name	rate	snake	awake
☐ pale	made	ape	safe	dare
scale	jade	cape	drake	fare
☐ gale	blade	gape	fake	plane
male	shade	grape	quake	vane

Long *e*

There are *very few* one-syllable words using long *e* in this spelling pattern.

☐ these   theme   here   mere   eve

Long *o*

☐	rope	bone	home	drove	nose
	hope	hone	dome	cove	prose
☐	cope	cone	rode	dove	stroke
	slope	prone	code	grove	scope
☐	remote	stone	pole	rove	bore
	dope	tone	hole	woke	wore
☐	lope	alone	stole	choke	globe
	pope	smoke	mole	coke	robe
☐	probe	chose	yoke	shore	more
	elope	those	broke	sore	store
☐	mope	hose	joke	spore	pose
	grope	close	poke	snore	sole

Long *i*

☐	hide	hive	file	dine	mine
	ride	dive	pile	wine	nine
☐	bide	five	mile	fine	time
	side	chive	tile	brine	rise
☐	slide	jive	vile	shine	tire
	wide	live	bite	thine	bribe
☐	glide	aside	kite	line	trite
	bride	inside	spite	tine	tribe
☐	chime	vine	fire	wife	stile
	slime	lime	wire	life	gripe
☐	dime	mime	hire	strife	pipe
	grime	prime	bite	fife	smile

Long *u*

In the following words, *u* represents either an /oo/ sound or a /yoo/ sound. You should tell the children that the consonant *y* is sometimes part of the long *u* sound.

☐	use	crude	fume	cube	rule
	fuse	rude	plume	pure	Yule
☐	abuse	nude	prune	cure	tube
	amuse	cute	dune	duke	fluke

Notes

Grade
Spelling Dictation

Reviewing short vowels with what has been taught so far

Begin the year by reviewing the consonants, the sequence of sounds, and short vowels. These reviews will give you the opportunity to assess the ability levels of your grade-two students. Children should be able to spell the whole word.

Short a

☐ stand	grasp	and	hand
clamp	camp	lamp	had
☐ draft	slant	sand	bat
plant	damp	sad	bad
☐ blast	grant	tramp	flat
ask	flap	blank	fast
☐ brand	band	drank	mast
trash	strap	thank	stamp
☐ ham	crab	ash	champ
blab	flash	cramp	stab
☐ crash	ban	drab	brash
can	slab	gash	clan

Short *e*

☐ spend	trend	pest	wet
blend	spend	chest	bet
☐ end	nest	jest	get
bend	west	test	jet
☐ lend	vest	left	let
mend	best	cleft	met
☐ tent	wed	fresh	send
went	shed	felt	elk
☐ bent	bled	melt	crest
sent	fed	them	rest
☐ dent	Fred	slept	invent
ten	sled	help	vent
☐ then	step	check	pet
net	tend	red	set

Short *i*

- [ ] drift   spit   drip   ink
  sift   split   skip   pink

- [ ] lift   lit   dip   stink
  swift   hit   slip   think

- [ ] shift   bit   trip   drink
  fist   fit   clip   slink

- [ ] list   flit   snip   mink
  mist   pit   tip   clink

- [ ] wind   lick   slim   thing
  twig   brick   thin   swing

- [ ] lint   trick   in   sling
  glint   slick   chin   spring

- [ ] hint   imp   blimp   fling
  mint   limp   chimp   sting

- [ ] crisp   crimp   tint   bring
  stick   shrimp   fin   king

Short *o*

❑ slop	chomp	chop	not
flop	lost	hop	cot
❑ cost	drop	clop	got
plop	trod	crop	hot
❑ plod	frost	pond	shot
shod	cost	romp	jot
❑ blot	lost	soft	lot
stop	shop	bond	slot
❑ pop	jog	frog	romp
prop	bog	log	stomp
❑ rot	frond	smog	fox
tot	clog	fond	blond
❑ flock	dog	bond	clomp
frock	fog	prod	odd
❑ clock	flog	Honda	off
stock	hog	on	mop

Short *u*

☐ hunt	just	drum	lump
bunt	trust	glum	slump
☐ punt	dust	gum	duck
runt	rust	plum	stuck
☐ hut	crust	clump	luck
shut	must	dump	truck
☐ shunt	trust	stump	cluck
blunt	gust	jump	chuck
☐ much	shush	gun	bunch
such	mush	slug	punch
☐ gush	plush	hug	lunch
hush	rush	bug	crunch
☐ brush	crush	rug	hunch
flush	sun	tug	munch
☐ slush	fun	plug	dusk
blush	bun	thump	tusk

Reviewing one- and two-syllable words and the word endings *er, ed, ing, y, es,* and *s* with the short vowels

Short *a*

☐ plants	blasting	rafter	grander	acting
planter	masts	after	bands	facts
☐ planting	past	drafty	casting	tact
sandy	casting	shafts	bath	plans
☐ pansy	vast	grants	math	hams
patsy	lasting	daft	path	ants
☐ handy	nasty	flanks	jams	glands
dandy	pantry	lanky	prams	ramps
☐ crafty	clasping	tramping	clasp	rang
thanks	gasping	cramping	apt	sang
☐ chanting	plaster	flask	hang	asking
ranking	grasped	masking	clang	basks
☐ tanker	crashing	flashy	slang	crab
pranks	rashes	clashing	bang	flab
☐ pants	trashy	crashing	fang	drab
slanting	cashing	thrash	gang	slab
☐ landing	camps	bashing	hangs	stabs
stands	camper	dashing	sprang	Brad
☐ hands	camping	lashing	cranking	scrams
plaster	damper	mashing	plans	banker
☐ faster	hamper	sashes	clans	Frank
canter	stamps	splashing	bans	blanks

Short *e*

- belts / gelding — slender / render — benches / drenching — bending / empty — frenzy / lends
- welding / sending — wending / tents — enemy / ending — mending / smelter — French / felt
- western / pelting — melted / vending — renting / extra — vespers / camel — Denver / tender
- smelting / melding — flexing / spending — denting / hexing — tending / westerner — zesty / petal
- rests / jesting — fresher / meshing — fleshy / stench — medal / pedal — entry / twenty
- lest / nesting — helper / shelf — steps / swept — trembling / very — dented / spent
- pester / testing — elfin / Welsh — lefty / hefty — plenty / tempest — rents / herself
- venting / best — pesky / desks — held / vexing — kept / kelp — bets / tenting
- vests / creating — shelter / presto — deftly / swelter — text / blemish — hems / hens
- tester / lest — temper / tempting — member / Dexter — render / never — Fred / weds
- trends / blender — fester / depths — detect / inject — trends / smelts — then / protest
- sent / fender — tenth / sleds — protect / subject — self / myself — object / ever

Short *i*

☐ thrifty	impy	fishy	slips	lifting
swiftly	skimpy	flimsy	stilted	sifter
☐ nifty	shrimps	brims	shifting	clips
stinker	chimps	hinting	ships	windy
☐ blinker	blimps	grinch	tipsy	hinder
winking	limping	flinty	fifty	tinder
☐ thinking	wimpy	glinting	nifty	wispy
himself	wintry	linty	visit	crispy
☐ silky	slinky	sprinter	clinker	figs
milking	tinker	printer	drinking	wins
☐ tilts	bids	minty	gilded	fins
risky	fibs	tinted	spindly	tins
☐ frisky	sits	wilted	dwindling	wits
brisk	bibs	simply	kindling	thins
☐ inky	digs	tilts	crisper	spits
pinky	whimper	jilted	inkling	wigs
☐ listing	swishing	lilting	tinkling	sixty
misty	wished	whisker	sprinkling	mixing
☐ sister	crimping	brisker	shrinks	dishes
twisty	fishing	whisper	living	hilt
☐ blister	inching	rigs	disks	giving
fist	dims	filthy	crinkling	sliver
☐ drifting	swims	richer	shiver	filming
drifter	sins	listing	liver	lisping

Short *o*

- ☐ romper   frosty   songster   fondling   lofty
  stomping   joshing   longing   golfing   fonder

- ☐ chomped   sloshing   blonder   body   shots
  clock   topsy   promptly   spots   ponds

- ☐ pomp   Flopsy   responding   often   slots
  ponder   dropsy   softer   bonding   trots

- ☐ lost   proper   bother   plots   cloth
  costing   prosper   golfer   clots   froth

- ☐ stronger   stops   socks   fondly   Congo
  longer   crops   rocky   blond   yonder

- ☐ longest   blots   locket   cods   pronto
  offers   flops   pocket   lofty   conch

- ☐ gongs   globs   docking   comet   poncho
  thongs   snobs   shocker   upon   closet

- ☐ throngs   chops   mocking   got   fronds
  songs   shops   rocker   blot   gosling

- ☐ frosting   frothy   blocking   docking   gosh
  rots   moths   clocks   jots   stocky

- ☐ honking   broth   frocks   posh   foxy
  softer   lobster   flocking   galoshes   boxing

- ☐ crofter   mobster   smocks   drops   agony
  lofts   cloth   rocketing   rocking   props

- ☐ fostering   costing   socket   convent   tops
  belongs   stocking   rocking   content   throbs

Short *u*

☐ lumpy   jumbo   crushing   bumbling   sprung
   bumpy   stunts   mushy   stumbling   rung

☐ stumps   runty   hush   fumbling   hung
   rumps   number   slushy   grumbling   sung

☐ dusty   slumber   rushes   rumbling   stung
   dumpling   hunting   gushing   tumbling   spuds

☐ punts   plush   plunder   crumpling   funds
   rusty   shunting   slush   blustering   brunt

☐ grumpy   bunting   brushing   thumping   musty
   crusty   crunchy   thrush   crumpet   bunts

☐ lunches   trumpet   grunted   bunching   lusty
   mumps   gulping   punches   blunts   brunch

☐ luster   gulch   pulpy   dumping   plugs
   fluster   mulch   under   clumping   thugs

☐ blunder   cluster   such   pumping   struts
   lumber   duster   bulk   fungus   slums

☐ slugs   just   sulky   thrust   strums
   nuts   must   hulks   chunky   trunks

☐ puns   busts   bulbs   spunky   bunks
   nuns   gusty   strung   bunker   slumps

☐ bugs   trusty   slung   clunker   husky
   clubs   thus   lung   drunk   gulfs

☐ cubs   bunching   flung   junking   stubs
   grubs   hunch   clung   plunking   shuns

Teaching words with short vowels followed by *r*

With each of the vowel-*r* combinations, tell the children to spell the sound as they hear it: /er/=*er*, /ar/=*ar*, /ir/=*ir*, /or/=*or*, /ur/=*ur*. You may wish to dictate eight *er* words on one day, followed by eight *ar* words the next day, followed by *ir* words, and so on, returning to *er*, *ar*, and so on, as needed.

er

☐ perch	perfect	stern	verb
berth	servant	Vern	superb
☐ herb	clerk	alert	filbert
fern	serpent	Bert	insert
☐ serf	perky	pert	lantern
her	herd	western	cavern
☐ herself	person	tavern	superman
jerk	term	sperm	filter

ar

☐ bark	arm	cargo	parchment
start	cart	alarm	pardon
☐ starchy	park	hard	Mars
lark	scarf	spark	harm
☐ bars	barter	scars	sharp
charm	cars	partner	darling
☐ barb	chart	afar	charming
harmful	harp	jars	starter

more ☞

- ☐ sharpener | parch | sharp | charter
  sparkling | shark | part | par

- ☐ tar | farther | gargling | Martha
  art | army | barter | remarking

- ☐ harsh | dart | party | carpenter
  upstart | marsh | tart | darting

- ☐ impart | snarling | march | yard
  artist | sharpen | garland | smart

- ☐ card | garden | bartender | garnet
  Denmark | lard | charting | apart

- ☐ garment | remark | hardy | harming
  apartment | parson | marbling | farm

- ☐ harder | depart | marlin | snarl
  barn | hardest | department | marmalade

- ☐ sarcastic | yarn | harken | stardom
  harpoon | tarnish | darn | farmer

- ☐ embark | jargon | varnish | ark
  harden | carton | Spartan | darning

- ☐ bark | barking | alarming | cartoon
  armful | dark | sharper | hardly

or

- ☐ ford | orbit | morning | sorting
  scorch | fort | hornet | escort

- ☐ snorting | porch | acorn | major
  protector | resort | perform | short

- ☐ shorter | forest | retort | forth
  sport | forbid | torch | adoring

- ☐ sort | torpedo | border | factor
  worn | snort | fork | forgot

- ☐ manor | dormant | cork | pork
  glory | tornado | factory | corny

- ☐ port | story | importer | pastor
  favor | form | record | florist

- ☐ normal | reporters | born | razor
  corner | instructor | order | storm

- ☐ inform | unborn | editor | northern
  thorn | reform | corker | inventor

- ☐ forum | corn | formal | thorny
  orders | orchard | horn | cormorant

- ☐ transform | reforming | organ | morn
  forget | shortening | portly | doctor

- ☐ torn | format | minor | reportedly
  ornament | scorn | important | selector

- ☐ import | shorn | monitor | forty
  escalator | forever | export | cord

- ☐ normal | former | ivory | torment
  north | lordly | performer | Gordon

more ☞

☐ humorist   dorm   sporting   shorten
chortling   organizing   York   informal

☐ deform   adornment   lordship   stork
shortly   elevator   informant   report

ir

☐ bird   birth   quirk   smirch
third   girth   skirt   firm

☐ first   mirth   sir   shirt
birch   squirt   dirt   shirk

☐ twirl   squirm   swirl   infirm
girl   whirl   smirk   catbird

☐ stir   dirk   chirp   astir
fir   flirt   thirsty   confirm

ur

☐ burst   purl   turf   burp
curd   furl   surf   blur

☐ curl   hurt   fur   purple
turn   lurch   lurk   blurt

☐ burn   churn   murky   curt
spurn   burl   Turkish   spurt

☐ hurl   curb   urn   burnt
church   furnish   slurp   turkey

Dictating sentences

Dictate sentences to the children approximately once a week having them practice what you have taught them in spelling, punctuation, and sentence structure.

1. Spelling

Dictate sentences using words, including doozers, that children should be able to spell.

The dogs barked as the children ran down the street.
On Sunday we had a fantastic time at the farm.
They went for a walk around the barnyard.

2. Punctuation

Dictate short sentences with appropriate emphasis to call for specific punctuation marks.

"Stop! Stop!" called the cop.
The big, fat, brown cat was sleepy.
What colors are the flowers?

3. Sentence Structure

Dictate two short sentences. Ask the children to decide where to put the capitals, periods, and question marks to indicate whole sentences.

I have a cat. His name is Tom.
What is your name? My name is _____.
Look out the window. What do you see?

Reviewing simple two-syllable words

The following words are ones the children should be able to spell correctly. Dictate four or five words a day.

❑ solid	transfer	contrast	forbid	until
❑ during	charming	party	music	daring
❑ fever	fifty	habit	format	detect
❑ select	moment	whisper	shadow	itself
❑ carpet	crisper	swelter	within	behind
❑ relax	broken	perfect	belong	invent
❑ superb	reply	began	admit	remind
❑ lantern	timber	invest	neglect	intern
❑ secret	trinket	after	hatred	herself
❑ given	morning	acting	himself	chosen
❑ direct	swiftly	demand	prevent	darling
❑ finish	regret	open	expect	anger
❑ embark	perhaps	expand	coldly	even
❑ reject	market	father	present	frozen
❑ contract	mother	contrast	person	forget
❑ farther	intend	export	brother	result
❑ pretend	linger	upset	stolen	silent
❑ story	wagon	hundred	golden	study
❑ northern	token	duty	western	index

more ☞

- [ ] suspect   remark   resent   driven   permit
- [ ] inspect   select   driver   insist   credit
- [ ] tidy   tidbits   inform   prefer   omens
- [ ] later   subject   pony   protest   reflect
- [ ] result   exact   insist   simply   limit
- [ ] partner   number   singly   predict   object
- [ ] platform   cobweb   cabin   prospect   depend
- [ ] transmit   Latin   army   defend   visit
- [ ] butler   satin   splendid   waver   ugly
- [ ] broken   April   splendid   finders   taken

Reviewing two-syllable words with *er*

This is both a review of words with *er* endings and to make certain that children hear and use *er* in medial position (as in "alert," "convert," and so on).

☐ transfer winter	folder bumper	hinder holder	alert miser	over refer
☐ butler finger	fever fonder	anger thunder	fervent serpent	fender Peter
☐ linger never	hamper prefer	infer scraper	convert rarer	paper sister
☐ river enter	longer infer	stricter banter	diner bother	after trader
☐ super banker	grinder planter	filter crisper	modern herdsmen	permit driver
☐ tanker member	perfect master	stronger jerking	perform expert	fixer mixer
☐ monster liver	mister duster	spender silver	perhaps prosper	canter joker
☐ broker proper	refer under	bother safer	shelter singer	jester jumper
☐ umber grander	saver ever	prefer cavern	stinker dasher	tavern persist
☐ softer sprinter	lever tamper	quiver hermit	homer clever	wider liver
☐ diner closer	maker simpler	blunder lumber	twister hanger	tinder lobster
☐ whisper stapler	sampler dumper	finer jerky	printer monster	superb wafer

Teaching common spelling patterns

Common spelling patterns are when two or three letters are used to represent one or more spoken sounds. These lists are in no particular order. Teach them as needed.

ck

- ❑ pack   jack   trick   pocket
  back   lack   check   chick

- ❑ rack   clock   luck   flick
  sack   shack   deck   thick

- ❑ tack   quick   fleck   chicken
  crack   snack   neck   stick

- ❑ black   stack   huckster   kick
  flicker   slack   speck   brick

- ❑ snicker   block   rock   tuck
  wicker   click   thicken   truck

ic

- ❑ antic   romantic   basic   music
  frantic   hectic   magic   gothic

- ❑ plastic   cosmetic   chic   mimic
  aspic   magnetic   comic   metric

- ❑ spastic   poetic   cosmic   optic
  dramatic   athletic   electric   cubic

- ❑ picnic   epic   rustic   toxic
  tunic   relic   italic   public

le

- [ ] cable   idle   jumble   grumble
  table   bugle   mumble   temple

- [ ] able   dimple   stumble   staple
  sable   simple   ample   swindle

- [ ] fable   pimple   sample   stifle
  stable   tumble   nimble   rifle

- [ ] gable   crumble   bundle   triple
  noble   fumble   spindle   gamble

- [ ] maple   scramble   trample   angle
  single   people   tingle   spangle

g representing /j/

Tell the children that *g* sometimes represents the /j/ sound. Names such as George, Gillian, Gerry, and so on provide a good example. Have the children spell as much of the following words as possible.

- ❑ gem geometry gigantic gel
  geology gibe gelatin geography

- ❑ ginger gender geo margin
  gym germ gerbil gyro

- ❑ generate geranium gypsy genetic
  gentleman giant gentle generic

Tell the children that many words end with the /j/ sound, but never with the *j* letter. There are two common ways to spell /j/ at the end of a word.

ge representing /j/

- ❑ stage huge oblige large
  wage deluge barge urge

- ❑ sage refuge message enlarge
  cage forge enrage cartage

dge representing /j/

- ❑ budge badge judge fudge
  badger ledger fledge cudgel

- ❑ budget fridge trudge bridge
  ledge wedge sludge smudge

Teaching double consonant words

ll

☐ ball	bell	yell	swill
wall	well	shell	thrill
☐ fall	sell	smell	twill
tall	swell	bill	uphill
☐ stall	fell	fill	windmill
call	dwelling	kill	refill
☐ mall	jelly	skill	frill
recall	spell	still	chill
☐ drill	loll	golly	pill
mollusk	folly	shrill	dollar
☐ gull	filly	collar	hull
silly	hollow	bullet	chilly
☐ follow	jolly	skull	dull
hilly	dill	doll	holly

ss

- [ ] class   pass   less   gloss   hiss
  brass   overpass   mess   loss   kiss

- [ ] bass   underpass   press   moss   amiss
  fiberglass   bless   confess   toss   discuss

- [ ] grassd   impress   express   across   chess
  glass   excess   floss   stupidness   boss

- [ ] lass   dress   stress   fuss   cross
  mass   profess   unless   cuss   truss

ff

- [ ] bluff   scruffy   puff   cliff
  buff   gruff   stuffing   stiff

- [ ] cuff   huff   off   sniff
  miff   muffin   puffin   skiff

- [ ] tiff   buffet   offer   staff
  jiffy   huff   duffer   stuff

Teaching double consonant words with *er*

☐ shopper	manner	spatter	scanner	differ
cropper	teller	stammer	passer	offer
☐ supper	speller	wetter	stopper	killer
thinner	patter	butter	flipper	slipper
☐ tiller	filler	inner	tosser	gutter
stutter	thriller	skipper	planner	blotter
☐ flutter	kisser	hopper	manner	clipper
summer	shimmer	spotter	dropper	bitter
☐ better	blubber	matter	odder	setter
matter	glimmer	topper	buzzer	scatter
☐ hammer	litter	buffer	planner	winner
putter	presser	canner	butter	flatter
☐ latter	batter	sputter	sitter	seller
shutter	offer	slimmer	dresser	fatter
☐ runner	dimmer	mugger	scrubber	platter
letter	mutter	rubber	skimmer	hitter
☐ tripper	fitter	ladder	dinner	sinner
jogger	fritter	swimmer	bummer	miller
☐ logger	offer	shipper	quitter	banner
mudder	trimmer	muffler	whizzer	robber
☐ remitter	bladder	chopper	bigger	stiffer
rudder	splatter	speller	skitter	adder
☐ chatter	shatter	puffer	madder	rubber
glitter	slugger	grimmer	spinner	fodder

Teaching the *ng* spelling patterns

ang

- bang   fang   hang   mustang
  clang   rang   sang   tangy
- tang   twang   sprang   swang
  slang   boomerang   pang   yang

ing

- bring   spring   gardening   morning
  cling   string   evening   opening
- sing   swing   coloring   fasting
  fling   thing   covering   clinging
- king   wing   entering   singing
  sting   sling   gathering   mining

ong

- long   gong   prolong   along
  song   Hong Kong   sarong   longing
- tong   oblong   thong   belong
  strong   prong   throng   ding-dong

ung

- bung   lung   clung   stung
  flung   sung   hung   swung
- rung   unstrung   slung   unsung
  sprung   unhung

Teaching vowel sound patterns

The patterns of *oi* and *oy*

The difference between these vowel sounds is undistinguishable: *oi* is generally used in a medial position; *oy* is usually the ending of the root word.

oi

☐ oil	broil	rejoin	anoint
coil	avoid	loin	spoilt
☐ spoil	void	point	recoil
foil	tabloid	joint	devoid
☐ tinfoil	coin	exploit	choice
uncoil	join	moist	ointment
☐ boil	groin	hoist	rejoice
toil	enjoin	joist	voice

oy

☐ boy	employ	unemployed
soy	enjoy	troy
☐ coy	envoy	deploy
Joy	playboy	destroy
☐ Roy	royal	enjoyment
toy	loyal	employment
☐ ahoy	convoy	royalty
decoy	overjoy	loyalty

The pattern of *ow* as in *now*

❏ brown   how   cowl   flower
   clown   now   howl   tower

❏ crown   bow   fowl   bower
   down   cow   owl   power

❏ drown   pow   growl   towel
   frown   row   jowl   trowel

❏ gown   sow   prowl   vowel
   town   vow   yowl   howdy

The pattern of *ow* as in *snow*

❏ snow   low   shadow   thrown
   blow   bow   widow   flown

❏ crow   show   bowl   growth
   grow   slow   lowly   shadowy

❏ undertow   below   slowly   sown
   row   overthrow   blown   disown

❏ stow   glow   own   glowing
   flow   window   grown   blowing

The pattern of *ou* as in *out*

- [ ] out   couch   ground   pout
  foul   crouch   bound   dug-out

- [ ] noun   loud   found   about
  ouch   aloud   hound   scout

- [ ] pouch   cloud   pound   trout
  grouch   proud   sound   snout

- [ ] vouch   shroud   south   spout
  slouch   round   mouth   shout

The pattern of *ous* to sound /us/

- [ ] gorgeous   monstrous   hilarious   amorous
  monotonous   luminous   glamorous   obvious

- [ ] delicious   dangerous   vicious   glamorous
  humorous   thunderous   furious   tedious

Reviewing what has been taught so far

Regularly phonetic words to use to practice consonants and vowels

- ☐ tablet   control   edit   local   profit
  subject   benefit   credit   instruct   finest

- ☐ bundling   problem   outlet   depict   result
  insult   open   inflect   event   focus

- ☐ habit   contest   direct   depend   basis
  visit   maximum   protect   prospect   extend

- ☐ protect   finest   memo   president   soda
  program   begin   product   element   omit

- ☐ rewind   select   adopt   demand   expect
  revert   menu   even   elegant   exact

- ☐ invent   satin   content   lapel   seven
  invest   depend   admit   profit   eleven

- ☐ dining   moment   submit   patron   limit
  itself   until   husband   brunch   level

- ☐ himself   stipend   destruct   splendid   oldest
  hotel   strict   defend   Roman   motel

- ☐ taxing   dumping   fact   district   bonus
  result   unit   revolt   distinct   printer

- ☐ reflect   inspect   musical   index   brand
  respond   respect   constant   moment   deduct

- ☐ proper   complex   insect   apartment   object
  catalog   indirect   seventh   upsets   compliment

- ☐ given   develop   student   resist   refresh
  final   pilot   sixth   ninth   ferment

Teaching long vowels

Long vowels are perhaps the most difficult spelling patterns to learn. Children must be taught that frequently more than one letter is used to represent one sound and that there are several patterns that represent each long vowel sound.

The old rule, "When two vowels go walking, the first one does the talking," is right less than fifty percent of the time. Many common words, *said, look, steak, brought, chief, piece, bread, piano, caught, taught, break,* and so on do not follow the rule. The old rule, "The *e* on the end of the word makes the vowel up front say its name," is equally wrong. Consider *come, have, done, some,* and so on. Teaching children such rules frustrates them because the rules are certainly not reliable. We teach children the common spelling patterns for long vowels, which seems to work without creating problems in reading or spelling.

Teach long vowels as *ways to spell a sound.* The children will already know the names of each vowel. Introduce the name as the long vowel sound and then brainstorm for words that contain the sound. As the children think of words that contain long *a,* record the words on the chalkboard and on cards. Classify the words as to how the vowel sound is spelled, *ai* as in wait, *a-e* as in late, *et* as in filet, *eigh* as in sleigh, or *ei* as in vein.

Linguists have identified twenty-nine ways to spell long /a/. In the early grades you will find the most common spellings are *a-e, ai, a* alone and *ay.* Practice the most common spelling patterns. As children find other spellings for long /a/, recognize them, list them perhaps, but do not practice them. Allow children to generalize from the brainstormed lists. Ask, "When you say *a* on the end of the word, how will you likely spell it?"

Children may also cut out pictures that represent long *a* words. These can be pinned to a bulletin board with the spelling of the word attached to the picture.

more ☞

This may be a good time to introduce homonyms: those words that sound the same but are spelled differently to reflect different meanings, such as *pain* and *pane* and, of course, *to, too,* and *two.* Children enjoy collecting homonyms as they find them in their brainstorming sessions or in their daily writing and reading. You can help the children learn the various meanings, and this may be a good time to introduce a simple dictionary to the class.

In the following pages of long vowel dictation, we have added variations such as *ing, ed, est, ce, age,* and *ful.* These words should only be dictated if the children have already been taught these patterns.

Teaching long *a* vowel patterns

ai spelling long /a/

☐ tail rail	taint waif	derail detail	saint against	braid raid
☐ pail aid	restrain flair	wait restrain	contain inlaid	again paid
☐ fail frail	air chair	pertain maintain	dainty avail	bait paint
☐ jail quail	laid stair	sustain complain	unfair repair	quaint faint
☐ brain chain	pair hair	entertain explain	chairman mainly	retail retain
☐ rain strain	hairy fairy	unpaid postpaid	mailman complaint	detain remain
☐ painter plain	dairy disdain	repaid restraint	impair exclaim	refrain waist
☐ pain main	domain aim	unfair repair	failing sailing	claim maim
☐ Spain sprain	drain snail	despair airline	prevail brainstorm	waiter obtain
☐ container sustain	hail faith	airway daisy	ungainly aircraft	stain train
☐ grain slain	railroad wail	raisin tailor	remaining unchained	trail regain

a-e spelling long /a/

❑ brake	hate	pave	pace	invade
bake	plate	stave	dedicate	space
❑ cake	late	evade	meditate	race
lake	compare	engrave	disgrace	rate
❑ flake	crate	forgave	grace	decade
rake	slate	safe	brave	impale
❑ drake	ate	taste	migrate	trace
fake	spade	waste	place	erase
❑ lane	trade	age	sale	female
remake	fade	rage	gave	parade
❑ lace	grade	page	indicate	dale
stale	made	stage	fabricate	gale
❑ scale	wade	decorate	inflame	male
James	ape	cage	pale	inflate
❑ tame	grape	gage	tale	unsafe
came	drape	enrage	prepare	whale
❑ parkade	shape	sage	separate	declare
lame	tape	fare	became	fanfare
❑ game	cane	stare	operate	locate
fame	Zane	flare	donate	imitate
❑ dame	Jane	aware	interstate	deflate
blame	eliminate	pane	snare	beware
❑ flame	insane	care	estimate	debate
frame	plane	dare	rotate	escape
❑ shame	make	sake	take	wake
grave	spare	elate	cultivate	shave

ay spelling long /a/

☐ pay | Sunday | airway | tray | day
Friday | always | May | say | display

☐ archway | bray | ashtray | pathway | may
today | lay | relay | betray | belay

☐ Fay | prepay | bluejay | dismay | gay
leeway | byway | inlay | freeway | hay

☐ cutaway | replay | jay | interplay | foray
swaying | sprayed | skidway | gangway | Kay

☐ ray | delay | halfway | grayest | way
crayon | highway | rayon | grayish | sway

☐ holiday | prayer | crayfish | mainstay | slay
stayed | stay | haystack | midway | frayed

☐ spray | payday | Norway | playing | stray
overlay | outlay | decay | payment | clay

☐ outstay | underway | bay | portray | layer
waterway | parlay | railway | workday | fray

☐ gray | maybe | speedway | yesterday | play
astray | subway | naysay | pray | away

Teaching long *e* vowel patterns

e-e spelling long /e/

☐ these	grebe	adhere	Swede	here
eke	ampere	sincere	extreme	theme
☐ cashmere	insincere	eve	convene	Irene
Chinese	Steve	gangrene	interfere	mede
☐ Japanese	serene	Pete	Cantonese	mere
intervene	persevere	Maltese	Nazarene	theme
☐ severe	recede	precede	athlete	replete
intervene	compete	secrete	obsolete	obese
☐ complete	submarine	concrete	impede	delete
stampede	evening	Siamese	supreme	deplete

ee spelling long /e/

❏ bee	feet	degree	banshee	sleep
tree	beet	meek	carefree	sheep
❏ see	meet	tweet	chimpanzee	steep
fee	seep	sweet	disagree	deep
❏ free	sheet	freezing	employee	weep
glee	sleet	sneezing	keel	sweep
❏ flee	greet	cheering	pioneer	keep
agree	creep	greeting	velveteen	peep
❏ need	reef	chickadee	seem	peer
weed	beef	cheeky	garnishee	veer
❏ deed	jeep	deer	goatee	sneer
feed	street	agreement	Halloween	seen
❏ freed	screech	keeper	jamboree	teepee
heed	queen	keeping	jubilee	esteem
❏ seed	discreet	sleeping	oversee	teen
steed	been	teeth	referee	speech
❏ speed	green	between	hayseed	eel
bleed	sheen	week	linseed	feel
❏ creed	fleet	peek	cogwheel	creel
tweed	beer	seek	redeem	peel
❏ greed	steer	sleek	sixteen	steel
breed	velveteen	creek	fifteen	cheek
❏ heel	asleep	leeks	unseen	sheer
breeder	sweeper	reek	umpteen	cheer

ea spelling long /e/

☐ beat	clearly	creak	reach	rear
seat	peas	leak	heater	spear
☐ meat	beard	peak	cheater	tear
heat	bean	beak	beater	clear
☐ neat	clean	freak	neater	smear
peat	glean	weak	bleating	weary
☐ feat	jeans	speaker	eastern	dreary
pleat	lean	squeak	nearest	bleary
☐ treat	mean	leap	defeat	real
bleat	wean	heap	retreat	steal
☐ wheat	unclean	cheap	dreamer	meal
cheat	cream	sea	creamery	teak
☐ yeast	stream	flea	dealers	heal
beast	dream	reap	shear	peal
☐ feast	team	plea	leaf	seal
least	steam	tea	sheaf	deal
☐ east	beam	beneath	creamer	bleak
ear	gleam	underneath	ream	easing
☐ year	seam	sheath	leaving	greasy
dear	streamer	peach	weaving	reason
☐ fear	read	treason	reveal	preach
gear	bead	season	preacher	teach
☐ hear	lead	defeat	meanest	beach
near	plead	mistreat	featuring	each

ie spelling long /e/

☐ shriek	belief	spiel	movie
fief	relief	unbelief	sharpie
☐ field	brief	priest	rookie
shield	chief	handkerchief	cookie
☐ windshield	grief	fierce	Dixie
yield	kerchief	pierce	believed
☐ infield	thief	lassie	achieved
afield	relief	Lorie	grieve
☐ fiend	pansies	ponies	duties
piece	reveries	Indies	rubies
☐ thieve	charities	pigmies	economies
retrieve	peonies	remedies	fairies
☐ disbelieve	nineties	series	fisheries
cavities	comedies	miseries	parties

Teaching long *i* vowel patterns

i-e spelling long /i/

☐ ride glide	bribe tribe	tile kite	quite despite	pine spine
☐ stride hide	pride side	bite smite	invite alike	vine gripe
☐ bride slide	jibe dive	spite sprite	desire unite	ripe stripe
☐ tide wide	drive five	rise wise	entire provide	snipe pipe
☐ time dime	alive hive	dire fire	astride preside	strike file
☐ grime chime	chives thrive	finite hire	divide Yuletide	mile Nile
☐ lime slime	rife wives	desire tire	empire incline	pile vile
☐ mime prime	wife life	wire vampire	crocodile bile	inside arise
☐ brine dine	spike porcupine	wipe unlike	bedside swipe	feline besides
☐ fine shine	hike bike	valentine iodine	combine define	tripe entire
☐ thine line	dike like	lined excite	shoreline bagpipes	refine quite
☐ mine nine	Mike pike	mobile size	describe aspire	wise devise

igh spelling long /i/

❑	high	slight	sighing	sprightly	sight
	sigh	bright	lighting	rightly	tight
❑	right	brighter	brightly	might	plight
	fright	fighting	foresight	fight	flight
❑	frighten	lightning	blight	tighten	light
	mighty	twilight	Dwight	slightly	night
❑	thigh	insight	airtight	frightening	lighten
	brighten	limelight	goodnight	downright	delight
❑	skylight	highest	moonlight	midnight	aright
	overnight	candlelight	sunlight	outright	nigh

ie spelling long /i/

Remind the children that this was also a way to spell long *e*.

❑	die	vies	amplified	justified	necktie
	pie	flies	complied	pried	ties
❑	lie	cries	purified	fortifies	defied
	magpie	fireflies	stupefied	plies	denied
❑	supplies	lied	died	satisfied	lies
	tries	implied	dried	tied	untie
❑	petrified	sanctified	purified	replied	spied
	multiplied	intensified	gratifies	mortified	relied

Teaching long *o* vowel patterns

o-e spelling long /o/

☐ vote	lore	wove	arose	stone
note	sore	globe	expose	more
☐ rote	chore	robe	impose	bore
dote	wore	hole	enclose	core
☐ tote	quote	pole	dispose	store
code	crone	mole	disclose	shore
☐ rode	tone	sole	zone	pore
cone	drone	stole	ozone	fore
☐ bone	hose	galore	remote	froze
hone	chose	explore	erode	Rome
☐ those	nose	repose	smote	strove
throne	pose	abode	strobe	cove
☐ quote	rose	spoke	parole	cloves
choke	close	gore	explode	grove
☐ broke	home	snore	deplore	rove
smoke	dome	adore	invoke	stove
☐ joke	tore	remote	microbe	denote
alone	rope	scone	wardrobe	devote
☐ lone	cope	stoke	episode	decode
stroke	promote	implore	forebode	remote
☐ woke	hope	before	postpone	ashore
yoke	lope	restore	sunstroke	ignore
☐ shone	slope	awoke	propose	bloke
prone	mope	provoke	console	repose

oa spelling long /o/

- [ ] coat · soap · afloat · outboard · overboard · toad · load · bloat · boat · roam
- [ ] inboard · starboard · foam · approach · float · goat · coasting · oats · oath · coal
- [ ] throat · soar · oar · goal · foal · shuffleboard · moat · gloat · pasteboard · road
- [ ] inroad · boar · speedboat · roast · boast · board · aboard · shipboard · oaths · loaf
- [ ] toast · poach · coach · uproar · roaming · Joan · cupboard · topcoat · coast · blackboard
- [ ] roam · seafoam · dashboard · moan · loan · foamy · afloat · coaches · abroad · hoard
- [ ] groan · gloat · soapy · charcoal · poaches · lifeboat · oak · gunboat · switchboard · soak
- [ ] motorboat · floater · steamboat · croak · overcoat · rowboat · buckboard · cardboard · cloak · loaves
- [ ] redcoat · groaning · sailboat · billboard · clapboard · waistcoat · moaning · scapegoat · oaf · goad

ow spelling long /o/

- ❏ bow   bowl   slow   grown   blow
     lowly   know   thrown   flow   narrow

- ❏ snow   shown   grow   slowly   row
     show   blown   tow   follow   overthrown

- ❏ crow   own   stow   gallows   glow
     disown   below   overgrown   low   flown

- ❏ growing   bungalow   snowy   window   pillow
     slowest   snowing   widow   rowing   willow

- ❏ blower   overflow   crows   billow   elbow
     glowing   shadow   towing   rainbow   lower

- ❏ towrope   aglow   lowest   overthrown   yellow
     growth   shows   scarecrow   mellow   sorrow

o followed by *ld* spelling long /o/

- ❏ old   hold   untold   blindfold   told
     scold   resold   foothold   mold   golden

- ❏ scolding   foretold   holding   tenfold   fold
     manifold   gold   folded   behold   uphold

- ❏ sold   olden   marigold   withhold   bold
     colder   stronghold   folder   cold   retold

o followed by *lt* spelling long /o/

- ❏ bolt   bolted   voltage   volts   colt
     molting   revolt   molted   molt   thunderbolt

Teaching long *u* vowel patterns

u-e spelling long /u/ or /oo/

This spelling pattern can represent the sound /yoo/ or the sound /oo/. As *y* and *oo* are also used to represent these speech sounds, this pattern is one of the more difficult for children.

☐ sure	future	dilute	misrule	brute
fluke	manure	excuse	ridicule	fume
☐ duke	exude	confuse	vestibule	prude
huge	compute	transfuse	profuse	prune
☐ June	extrude	refuse	reuse	mute
tune	impure	peruse	impute	dude
☐ rule	consume	repute	delude	spruce
mule	insure	refute	Neptune	truce
☐ dispute	include	resolute	rebuke	cure
institute	seclude	absolute	disuse	lure
☐ dune	constitute	conclude	parachute	ruse
tube	interlude	creature	tribute	figure
☐ lube	prelude	secure	feature	chute
Rube	intrude	picture	enclosure	astute
☐ cube	nature	introduce	salute	abuse
pure	endure	reduce	execute	amuse
☐ jute	crude	exposure	induce	endure
cute	plume	manicure	deduce	denude
☐ nurture	resume	mature	produce	use
injure	volume	pasture	exclude	fuse
☐ tribune	scripture	deluge	procure	Yule
perfume	lecture	refute	insecure	flute

Notes

Grade
Spelling Dictation

3

Reviewing the spelling learned so far

Begin grade three by reviewing the consonants, the sequencing of the sounds, short and long vowels, and some of the common spelling patterns.

Phonetic words

The following words are spelled as pronounced. Children can practice and review as you dictate them. There are twelve words per lesson.

- basket   combat   filmstrip   demon
  disgust   total   candid   diving
  vitamin   limpet   camera   extend

- consult   respond   depth   expand
  salad   bacon   talent   intend
  consist   hamlet   crimson   testing

- vital   elect   arisen   sunset
  compact   behind   napkin   silent
  trumpet   conflict   disposal   impact

- tuna   constant   potent   signal
  halibut   rental   detest   stop
  criminal   casket   panel   drifting

- instant   suspect   marigold   inching
  dental   focus   untold   enchant
  Spanish   distract   behold   pumpkin

- tomato   spoken   dragon   human
  Mexican   evil   wagon   robin
  cupid   taken   bantam   panel

- distant   golden   stimulus   including
  defendant   zero   defrost   wisest
  dependent   reprimand   distrust   French

Words with *er*

☐ faster   monster   Chester   pamper
   master   softer   limber   disaster
   plaster   fonder   smelter   remember

☐ planter   yonder   shelter   October
   hamper   ponder   under   September
   camper   longer   tinder   November

☐ rafter   stronger   forever   suspender
   spender   bluster   tiger   hover
   fender   duster   Peter   consider

☐ blender   hunter   anger   bewilder
   lender   lumber   proper   paper
   tender   jumper   temper   defender

☐ jester   cluster   butler   deliver
   fester   bumper   linger   prisoner
   helper   bunter   slender   timber

☐ blister   splinter   ever   together
   sister   ember   amber   beholder
   mister   blinder   gander   carpenter

☐ contender   sander   finger   publisher
   hinder   banter   winter   sandpaper
   thumper   Denver   printer   performer

☐ drifter   silver   pelter   sprinter
   planter   number   softer   remainder
   reminder   super   whisper   fixer

Words with *y*

❏ handy   dusty   wiry   foolishly   frosty
   candy   crusty   only   perfectly   fondly
   sandy   grumpy   scanty   enemy   softly

❏ crafty   silly   lumpy   spunky   costly
   dandy   jumpy   flunky   jelly   Monty
   hanky   rusty   frisky   lucky   body

❏ shanty   bumpy   corny   yucky   lofty
   nasty   gusty   thorny   ducky   sloppy
   hefty   sleepy   ornery   plucky   salty

❏ zesty   springy   stormy   fluffy   dusty
   plenty   baby   forty   stuffy   tingly
   twenty   tenderly   seventy   puppy   Tony

❏ pesty   spindly   tasty   guppy   trusty
   pesky   trimly   pastry   stubby   flashy
   lefty   kindly   scary   crunchy   chubby

❏ Wendy   wildly   Mary   strongly   tubby
   identity   nifty   blindly   orderly   holly
   windy   humanity   properly   folly   sulky

❏ stinky   distinctly   sultry   property   Molly
   misty   chilly   ability   dolly   simply
   fifty   probably   tiny   activity   Polly

❏ sixty   empty   directly   stupidly   spotty
   twisty   secondly   zany   elderly   bossy
   slinky   wintry   exactly   mossy   family

Words with *ing*

☐ cramping — jumping — spitting — depending
frosting — camping — rushing — fitting
selecting — chomping — stamping — flushing

☐ kissing — reflecting — prompting — landing
bumping — dipping — restricting — costing
handing — grumbling — missing — stretching

☐ bonding — romping — strangling — hunting
hissing — representing — lasting — blushing
dripping — dividing — stomping — tangling

☐ dusting — gripping — revolving — choking
bending — splashing — spotting — publishing
shedding — resting — smashing — stopping

☐ bedding — abandoning — tending — flashing
trotting — thundering — wetting — nesting
crashing — flopping — contacting — getting

☐ cresting — thrashing — shopping — trucking
letting — trembling — hopping — slashing
clucking — humming — jesting — itching

☐ crossing — chucking — hemming — testing
stitching — tossing — plucking — betting
limping — wishing — strumming — torching

☐ muttering — sifting — fishing — drumming
scorching — fluttering — swinging — tapping
slugging — blanching — littering — hinting

☐ slapping — stuffing — lunching — flittering
thinking — spelling — lurching — munching
puttering — drinking — dwelling — tugging

☐ crunching — chattering — lifting — pressing
puffing — perching — directing — twisting
dressing — sputtering — pinching — exacting

Words with *er* for "good spellers"

- [ ] personal | distemper | deserter | filtering
  - understand | converter | terminus | helicopter
  - universal | deliver | fervent | everything

- [ ] sternly | publisher | advertisement | eraser
  - reformer | jetliner | servant | impersonate
  - confer | discover | dismember | suspender

- [ ] consider | properly | misery | deserving
  - fingerling | computer | lateral | whispering
  - recover | consumer | fertilizer | Bernard

- [ ] camera | hanger | examiner | another
  - Alexander | funeral | polisher | deserting
  - interpret | anger | hovering | Roberta

- [ ] remember | hunger | superman | perfectly
  - government | vertical | reserving | trumpeter
  - interest | minerals | interesting | fluster

- [ ] perfect | perfectly | preserver | recover
  - superb | disaster | cluster | bluster
  - herself | reminder | modern | deserving

- [ ] property | presenter | fermenting | tenderizing
  - adviser | whenever | persistent | ruler
  - verdict | conserver | informer | finisher

- [ ] opener | imperfect | blistering | fisherman
  - every | foster | sampler | entering
  - traveler | alabaster | hindering | tolerant

- [ ] dispenser | condenser | imperfect | serpent
  - permanent | carpenter | northern | smoldering
  - sandpaper | terminal | westerly | suspender

- [ ] inserting | cucumber | tinkering | afternoon
  - together | everlasting | federal | midterm
  - defender | lantern | customer | eternal

Words with *ic*

- [ ] fabric   antic   microscopic   optic
      tonic   aspic   ironic   tropic
      plastic   spastic   supersonic   economic

- [ ] public   anemic   bubonic   music
      dramatic   politic   harmonic   titanic
      antagonistic   specific   melodic   majestic

- [ ] drastic   static   sardonic   artistic
      electric   rustic   Nordic   colic
      frantic   caloric   capitalistic   panoramic

- [ ] cosmic   republic   electronic   monastic
      cosmetic   astronomic   antiseptic   heraldic
      fantastic   democratic   ethnic   futuristic

- [ ] historic   mimic   gothic   satanic
      bionic   gigantic   humanistic   Hispanic
      topic   panic   diagnostic   Pacific

- [ ] Atlantic   metric   animalistic   Arabic
      arithmetic   organic   statistic   Baltic
      athletic   heroic   Panasonic   Slavic

- [ ] platonic   moronic   ballistic   traffic
      sonic   hectic   Coptic   attic
      prolific   acoustic   poetic   comic

Adding *d* or *ed*

☐ blame   convene   bribe   handle   time
    blamed   convened   bribed   handled   timed

☐ drone   name   rumble   choke   rule
    droned   named   rumbled   choked   ruled

☐ cure   cable   revere   tune   crane
    cured   cabled   revered   tuned   craned

☐ title   stampede   interfere   hope   cube
    titled   stampeded   interfered   hoped   cubed

☐ land   enthrone   fire   romp   shape
    landed   enthroned   fired   romped   shaped

☐ bottle   elope   blend   hike   use
    bottled   eloped   blended   hiked   used

☐ graze   hamper   smile   compete   pile
    grazed   hampered   smiled   competed   piled

☐ exit   stamp   rust   plaster   wilt
    exited   stamped   rusted   plastered   wilted

☐ dump   blast   enter   cheat   act
    dumped   blasted   entered   cheated   acted

☐ shunt   fluster   frost   chant   heat
    shunted   flustered   frosted   chanted   heated

Doubling the consonant before adding *ed*

- [ ] flap · sip · flip · skim · fret
  flapped · sipped · flipped · skimmed · fretted

- [ ] whiz · hop · hum · grin · net
  whizzed · hopped · hummed · grinned · netted

- [ ] mug · pen · spot · strut · flit
  mugged · penned · spotted · strutted · flitted

- [ ] sup · cram · chop · plan · rag
  supped · crammed · chopped · planned · ragged

Teaching changing *y* to *i* and adding *es* or *ed*

- [ ] duty · pigmy · cavity · bunny · try
  duties · pigmies · cavities · bunnies · tries

- [ ] fairy · forty · ninety · candy · lily
  fairies · forties · nineties · candies · lilies

- [ ] twenty · pansy · empty · ruby · pony
  twenties · pansies · emptied · rubies · ponies

- [ ] remedy · entry · study · mutiny · vary
  remedies · entries · studied · mutinied · varied

- [ ] amplify · marry · dry · weary · deny
  amplifies · married · dries · wearies · denies

- [ ] palsy · candy · curtsy · reply · fry
  palsied · candied · curtsied · replied · fried

- [ ] satisfy · imply · misery · justify · spy
  satisfied · implied · miseries · justified · spied

Teaching the *oo* spelling patterns

oo as in *look*

❑ wood   goody   outlook   mistook   hook
  woody   took   overlook   pothook   good

❑ hood   undertook   look   withstood   cook
  stood   crook   booking   unhook   wooden

❑ aloof   cooking   manhood   textbook   nook
  dogwood   hoodlum   flatfoot   underfoot   shook

❑ driftwood   book   afoot   sisterhood   looking
  brook   cookie   mistook   wildwood   lookout

oo as in *toot*

❑ roof   toot   uproot   tooth   booth
  soon   brood   spool   mushroom   lagoon

❑ bloom   tool   taproom   crooner   food
  shampoo   mood   coon   cartoon   boost

❑ bamboo   broody   croon   baboon   stoop
  igloo   cool   moon   macaroon   broom

❑ kangaroo   scoot   stool   teaspoon   pool
  kazoo   trooping   zoom   saloon   droopy

❑ skidoo   groom   dragoon   pontoon   drool
  shoot   root   boot   proof   spoof

Teaching the double *ll* patterns

all

☐ hall   befall   overall   waterfall   ball
   catcall   pitfall   squallcall   Cornwall   fall

☐ rainfall   softball   downfall   recall   mall
   baseball   eyeball   windfall   bookstall   tall

☐ footfall   forestall   wall   install   thrall
   enthrall   all   nightfall   small   stall

ull

☐ pull   bullet   sully   mullet   lull
   dull   cull   full   numskull   gullet

☐ seagull   hull   scull   pullet   mull
   bull   dully   bulletin   scullery   gully

ill

☐ filly   gorilla   sill   millet   pill
   miller   hillock   grill   caterpillar   till

☐ killer   thriller   vanilla   sillier   chilly
   pillow   willow   billowed   armadillo   billy

☐ illness   willing   filling   village   silly
   pillage   skillet   skillful   flotilla   villa

ell

- [ ] eggshell   telling   teller   propeller   sell
  cellar   dweller   jelly   belly   quell

- [ ] smelly   stellar   patella   Magellan   fell
  rubella   Cinderella   cowbell   inkwell   dell

- [ ] misspell   spelling   undersell   yellow   fellow
  mellow   bellow   barbell   bluebell   Kelly

Teaching the use of *tion* to spell /shun/

- [ ] notion / lotion — vacation / devotion — reservation / inflation — tradition / navigation
- [ ] potion / nation — promotion / condition — imitation / nutrition — motivation / sensation
- [ ] station / ration — invitation / donation — estimation / implication — rotation / graduation
- [ ] motion / emotion — isolation / petition — position / fumigation — formation / tuition
- [ ] meditation / lubrication — competition / obligation — civilization / duration — negation / elimination
- [ ] preservation / disposition — admiration / destination — edition / calculation — locomotion / jubilation
- [ ] superstition / recognition — condition / mutation — malnutrition / fashion — condensation / salvation
- [ ] substation / temptation — stimulation / transportation — hesitation / revelation — ignition / position
- [ ] presentation / composition — impersonation / petition — recognition / eradication — observation / identification
- [ ] fixation / reduction — quotation / reputation — fortification / composition — repetition / ambition
- [ ] caution / prohibition — speculation / tabulation — premonition / vexation — vibration / probation
- [ ] exposition / salutation — induction / vocation — organization / partition — publication / notation

Teaching prefixes and suffixes

When introducing or reviewing these affixes, teach and/or discuss their meaning and their effect on the root word.

able

Explain that *able* may be part of a root word, such as *stable*, or it may be added to a word to indicate "able to be," as in *pardonable*.

- table
  stable

  capable
  disable

  pardonable
  usable

- fable
  able

  enable
  durable

  teachable
  seasonable

- gable
  cable

  likable
  lovable

  probable
  readable

- sable
  timetable

  passable
  portable

  printable
  unstable

- desirable
  adorable

  incapable
  improbable

  constable
  detachable

- delectable
  reasonable

  incomparable
  navigable

  deplorable
  escapable

- punishable
  presentable

  perishable
  notable

  explicable
  valuable

- personable
  vegetable

  indispensable
  formidable

  removable
  unavoidable

be

- [ ] between / beyond — before / become — begone / befriend — beneath / because
- [ ] beside / below — berate / beware — bespoken / beginning — behold / belittle
- [ ] behave / beget — became / befall — betrothed / behind — believe / befuddle
- [ ] betwixt / beloved — belong / bedeck — beset / beseech — bestow / betoken

re

- [ ] redo / remember — refrain / reproduce — remake / restate — replant / resent
- [ ] remain / reuse — refried / reconsider — retell / reclaim — relent / recoil
- [ ] reread / repaint — replay / retain — repeat / rebuilt — retold / rewrite
- [ ] rewrite / reenter — reform / retake — repent / restart — refit / resell

dis

- [ ] dislike / dismiss — dispel / disturb — disrupt / dismember — discard / discontent
- [ ] disappear / distinct — dismantle / disgrace — disjointed / dissent — distaste / disconnect
- [ ] disfigure / disappoint — distinct / disdain — disbelief / discord — disclaim / display

auto

- [ ] automate
  - autocratic
  - autograph

automobile
autonomy
autopilot

automotive
autobiography
autonomy

un

- [ ] unfit
  - uncorked

underdog
until

ungrateful
untold

- [ ] unfriendly
  - unstick

undesirable
undercover

unwise
unprintable

- [ ] unable
  - inspect

unsold
under

undermined
unpleasant

- [ ] underpaid
  - unfold

unspeakable
unthinking

unpick
undependable

- [ ] uncover
  - uninformed

uncooked
unbend

unattended
unchained

uni

☐ unit	united	union	unite
unison	university	reunion	reunite
☐ universe	community	uniformity	unionist
unicorn	universal	unified	unify
☐ uniform	immunity	unification	unity
unilateral	communion	uniflow	unicycle

bi

☐ bicycle	bicorn	bifold	bible
bivalve	bifocal	biceps	biology
☐ bilateral	bipod	biplane	bipolar
binocular	bisect	bicuspid	biography

tri

☐ tricycle	triad	tripod	triangle
triple	tricolor	trident	trinity
☐ trillium	trio	tribunal	triplicate
triplets	triceps	trivet	triceratops

sub

- ❏ subway substandard submarine
  sublet sublime substitute

- ❏ subsist subsidy subordinate
  subtropical subdivide subnormal

- ❏ subtract subalpine subcontract
  submit subarctic subserve

- ❏ subplot suborbital subscribe
  subject submerge suburb

super

- ❏ superb superman superstrict
  supersafe superhuman superimpose

- ❏ supercargo supermarket supernatural
  supersaver superclass superpower

- ❏ superfine superheat supervalue
  superintend supersonic superficial

- ❏ superbold superstitious superintendent
  superstructure supervise supervisor

Appendix

Spelling Checklists

The checklists on pages 178–180 may be used to record each child's independent spelling ability. When a child has transferred what has been taught in daily dictation to everyday writing practice, it may be safely assumed that the child has learned what has been taught.

To keep a file of each child's writing for assessment, collect a sample of *independent* writing from each child every two weeks. At roughly four week intervals, compare the writing samples to the appropriate checklist. Enter the date beside the particular skill to indicate the child's learning. This can be an ongoing activity, rather than an assessment of all the children at one time. Doing two or three children a week will complete an average class in a twelve-week cycle.

GRADE ONE SPELLING CHECKLIST

_____
child's name

Date Learned

_____ Can use **M__**, **S__**, **F__**, **B__**, **T__**, **C__** correctly in both initial and final positions

_____ Can print correctly a three- or four-letter phonetic word using the short vowel **A** nd the consonants that have been taught

_____ Can use **R__**, **L__**, **P__** correctly in both initial and final positions

_____ Can print correctly three- or four-letter phonetic words using the short vowel **O** and the consonants that have been taught

_____ Can use **D__**, **G__**, **N__**, **W__** correctly in both initial and final positions

_____ Can print correctly three- or four-letter phonetic words using the short vowel **I** and the consonants that have been taught

_____ Can use **H__**, **J__**, **K__**, **V__** correctly in both initial and final positions

_____ Can print correctly three- or four-letter phonetic words using the short vowel **U** and the consonants that have been taught

_____ Can print correctly three- or four-letter phonetic words using the short vowels **A__**, **O__**, **I__**, **U__** with the consonants learned so far

_____ Can use **Y__**, **Qu__**, **Z__** correctly in initial position only

_____ Can use **Qu__** in initial or medial position

_____ Can use **X__**, **Z__** correctly in final position only

_____ Can print correctly three- or four-letter phonetic words using the short vowel **E** and the consonants that have been taught

_____ Is beginning to discern the difference between short **e** and short **i**

_____ Can write a one-syllable purely phonetic word correctly

_____ Can use consonant blends in both initial and final positions

_____ Can write a two-syllable purely phonetic word correctly

_____ Can write three- and four-syllable phonetic words correctly

_____ Can use the word endings **s__**, **ing__**, **y__**, **er__** correctly when the root word requires no change

_____ Can use the digraphs **sh__**, **th__**, **ch__** in initial and final positions

_____ Has been introduced to the long vowel sounds and indicates learning by spelling the long /a/ sound as **a-e__**, the long /e/ sound as **e-e__**, the long /i/ sound as **i-e__**, the long /o/ sound as **o-e__**, and the long /u/ sound as **u-e__**

_____ Can use the standard spelling forms of the following words: **the__**, **was__**, **here__**, **one__**, **said__**, **they__**, **come__**, **saw__**, **you__**, **of__**, **is__**, **who__**

GRADE TWO SPELLING CHECKLIST

_____
child's name

Date Learned

_____ Uses consonants correctly in both initial and final positions

_____ Uses consonants in correct sequence

_____ Can use the short vowels a___, e___, i___, o___, u___ correctly in phonetic words of one syllable

_____ Can discern the difference between the short vowels e and i in words of one syllable

_____ Can write correctly phonetic words of two syllables using short vowels

_____ Can add the word endings y___, s___, ing___, ly___, er___, ed___, es___ to the ends of words if the word form does not change

_____ Can use the consonant digraphs ch___, th___, sh___ correctly in both initial and final positions

_____ Can use correctly the vowel dipthongs er___, ar___, or___, ir___, ur___

_____ Can use correctly the vowel dipthongs oi___, oy___

_____ Can use correctly the spelling patterns ow as in now___, ow as in $snow$___, ou as in out___, ous as /us/___

_____ Can use correctly the spelling patterns ang___, ing___, ong___, ung___

_____ Can use correctly the spelling patterns ck___, ic___, le___

_____ Can use correctly the spelling patterns g as /j/___, ge as /j/___, dge as /j/___

_____ Can use correctly double consonant words using ll___, ss___, ff___

_____ Indicates awareness that in words containing two or more syllables, a short vowel is usually followed by more than one consonant while a long vowel is usually followed by one consonant

_____ Can add the word endings s___, ly___, ed___, es___, y___, ing___, er___ when the basic word form changes

_____ Is aware of the most common spelling patterns inherent in words with long vowels

_____ Can discern the long vowel sound and use one of the spelling patterns for each sound:
  long /a/ : ai___, $a\text{-}e$___, ay___
  long /e/: ee___, ea___, $e\text{-}e$___, ie___
  long /i/: $i\text{-}e$___, igh___, ie___
  long /o/: $o\text{-}e$___, oa___, ow___, old___, olt___
  long /u/: $u\text{-}e$___

_____ Shows awareness that different ways of spelling the same sound often indicate a change in word meaning

_____ Can spell correctly the common non-phonetic words: $because$___, $have$___, $again$___, are___, $were$___, $would$___, $should$___, $could$___

GRADE THREE SPELLING CHECKLIST

_____
child's name

Date Learned

_____ Can spell correctly one-syllable words containing a short vowel sound

_____ Can use the digraphs *ch___, th___, sh___* correctly in initial, final, and medial positions

_____ Can use consonant blends in initial, final, and medial positions

_____ Can add the word endings *s___, er___, ing___, y___ , ly___, ed___, es___* when not required to change the basic word form

_____ Is acquiring skill in correct usage of the long vowel spelling patterns for the following:
long /a/ : *ai___, ay___, a-e___, eigh___*
long /e/: *ea___, ee___, ie___, e-e___*
long /i/: *i-e___, igh___, ie___*
long /o/: *oa___, o-e___, ow___, oe___, old___, olt___*
long /u/: *ue___, u-e___, ew___*

_____ Indicates an awareness of homonyms. Realizes that to change the meaning of a word, one must often change the spelling

_____ Can write correctly two- and three-syllable words that are totally phonetic

_____ Indicates awareness that in words containing two or more syllables, a short vowel is usually followed by more than one consonant while a long vowel is usually followed by one consonant

_____ Can correctly add the following word endings to *all* words:
y___, ing___, s___, er___, est___, ly___

_____ Is acquiring skill in changing word forms from singular to plural by adding *s___* or *es___* or by changing the *y* to *i* and adding *es___*

_____ Is acquiring skill in changing word forms from present tense to past tense by adding *d___* or *ed___* or by changing *y* to *i* and adding *ed___*

_____ Can correctly use *tion* to spell /*shun*/

_____ Can use the vowels digraphs *er___, ar___, or___, ir___, ur___, oi___, oy___, au___, aw___, ow___, ou___, short oo___, long oo___, all___, ull___, ill___, ell___*

_____ Is developing the ability to spell and use with meaning the suffix *able___* and prefixes *re___, dis___, un___, uni___, bi___, tri___, be___, sub___, super___, auto___*

_____ Spells correctly simple compound words

_____ Is developing ability in spelling:
friend___, people___, tomorrow___, girl___, does___, off___, right___, write___, said___, when___, once___, their___, two___, too___

180   SPELLING THROUGH PHONICS

Dear Parents,

This year we are teaching spelling based on phonics. The students will learn the sounds of the consonants, the many ways the vowel sounds are written, and how to sequence letters in a word and words in a sentence.

Students will be writing every day, practicing their printing and spelling as well as they can. In their daily writing, they may try to spell hard words (just as they tried to say difficult words when they started to speak) and get them wrong. Some people call this invented spelling. I prefer to call it temporary spelling, and I will not be correcting these first efforts if they are beyond what has been taught. As the students are taught more, their spellings will become more nearly standard and, finally, correct. I will be encouraging them to write as much of a word as they can and will teach them how to do this. This will force them to practice the phonics they know, but I am aware that they will try to write words beyond their skill level. This letter is to assure you that "mistakes" are temporary and will be corrected in time.

As an example, a child may like the word 'gorgeous' and want to write it. '*Grjs*' is readable and indicates that the child has learned four separate consonant sounds and knows how to sequence them correctly. If I mark this wrong and ask the child to correct it, I am asking the impossible. (If the student spelled gorgeous '*grsj*', I would have her correct the error in sequencing.) As more phonics are learned, *grjs* may become *grjus*, or *gorjus*. When the spelling patterns *ge* to spell *j*, and *ous* to spell *us* are learned, the child will be able to spell gorgeous correctly. Children naturally want to do their best; as soon as new learning occurs, they quickly adapt to the change.

I hope this has given you a better understanding of temporary spelling. Please feel free to call me at _____ if you would like to talk about this or obtain more information about our spelling program.

Sincerely,

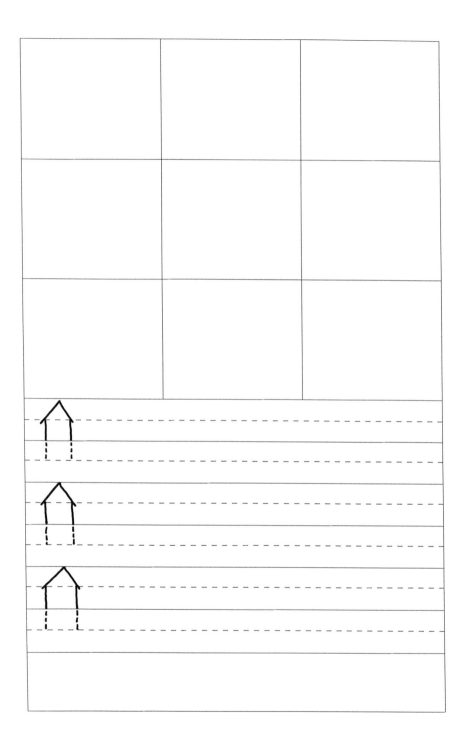

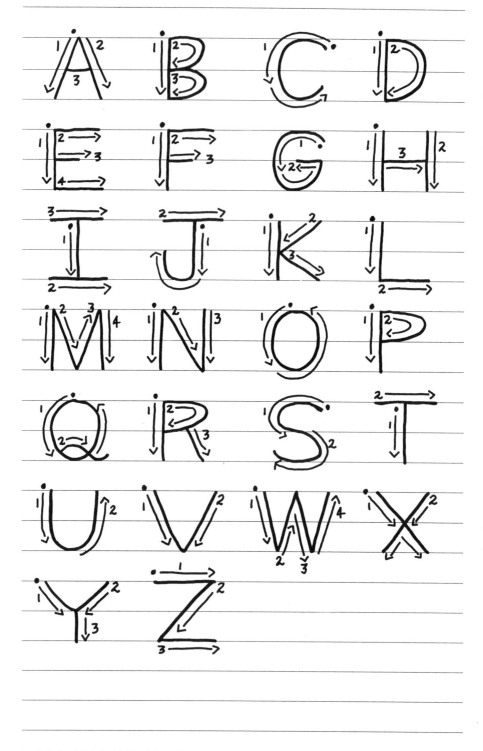